# GHOSTS
## The Illustrated History

Return this book on or before the last date

Peter Haining

# GHOSTS

## The Illustrated History

TREASURE PRESS

For
My son, Richard

'The man whose spirit hath none to care for it—
Thou and I have often seen such a one.'
*The Epic of Gilgamish*
2,000 B.C.


'I don't believe in God, but I do believe in
ghosts.'
John Huston
*In 1974, talking about*
*the eighteenth-century*
*ghost who haunts his*
*mansion in Galway,*
*Ireland*

Previous pages: Page 1:
One of several strange
pictures which have been
published in recent years of
'Christ figures' in the
clouds — this one was taken
by Robert Stull in Florida

Page 2: This picture of
a ghostly monk was taken by
the Rev. Kenneth F. Lord
in the Parish Church of
Skelton-on-Ure, Yorkshire

First published in Great Britain in 1974 by
Sidgwick and Jackson Limited

This edition published in 1987 by
Treasure Press
59 Grosvenor Street
London W1

Copyright © 1974 by
Peter Haining and Sidgwick and Jackson Limited

Design by Bob Burroughs
Picture research by Jonathan Moore

ISBN 1 85051 204 3

Printed in Czechoslovakia

50649

# Contents

|   |   | Page |
|---|---|---|
| 1 | Talking of Ghosts | 7 |
| 2 | Homage to the Spirits of the Dead | 15 |
| 3 | Poltergeists and Magicians | 25 |
| 4 | Phantom Drummers and Ghostly Warnings | 37 |
| 5 | The Cock Lane Ghost and Commonsense | 49 |
| 6 | Ghost Shows, Phantom Ships and the Birth of Spiritualism | 59 |
| 7 | Spirit Photographs – Real or Fake ? | 75 |
| 8 | Ghostly Phenomena Today | 97 |

## Ghost's exit through wall beats police net

By Martin Huckerby

A mysterious intruder was spotted in the dungeons of the Great Hall at Winchester yesterday, despite the stringent security precautions because of the London bomb trial taking place there.

The man, said to have been dressed in a three-cornered hat and a three-quarter length cutaway coat, apparently escaped the police security net by disappearing through a 2ft thick wall.

The apparition was reported to have been seen by a prisoner from Winchester prison who was on a working part[...] out of a cell in the dungeons under [...] century hall.

The prisoner, [...] not been released [...] staggered out of [...] collapsed. Later [...] the figure as a po[...] declared that he [...] appeared through [...] the cell. Officials w[...] posed to take his sto[...] ously, although on[...] thought that he ac[...] lieved that he had see[...]

A spokesman at W[...]

## Golf club's bogey rattles a family

THE strange goings-on at a 300-year-old golf clubhouse are unnerving steward Mr. George Webster and his wife, Sheila.

They are convinced "something" is watching them and their two sons at West Bowling Golf Club, Bradford, Yorks.

Mr. Webster, 48, said: "One night I distinctly heard snooker balls clicking about on table, but when I in they were all in pockets."

Club member David Cockcrof Menston, near said: "I went in snooker room on As I was leaving clicking and s balls moving a the table.

"I was not f but [...] ; unus [...] plain

## Killer's ghost asks to be forgiven

By Daily Mail Reporter

A GHOST which has been terrifying the families of two sailors has been identified.

It is said to have [...] itself to a [...]

Philip Llewellyn, [...] main-

[...] at [...] ill [...] ve [...] ri-

[...] ave [...] rom [...] mes [...] mell. [...] hout

[...] have [...] call in [...] stigate [...] out."

## WARNING OF A PUB GHOST

EX-LANDLORD Tom Ward turned up ag[...] for an eerie midnight meeting in the ce[...] of his old pub.

He slipped out of the shadows, pale and h[...] gave a grim warning to the [...] and [...] er. 31-year-old Brian Withington. [...] the old landlord had die [...] before. After his [...]

## Spectre of dead wife led stowaway to leap into sea

Dubai, June 15.—An Englishman rescued from the Atlantic off West Africa told reporters today of how he jumped from a ship into the ocean after thinking he saw his dead wife in the water.

Mr Lawrence John Ellis, aged 31, said he stowed away in a container ship at Liverpool with a friend on May 15 because he was anxious to get to Australia where his wife had died last December.

He and his companion were allowed to work in the ship after being discovered, but he "became very depressed" thinking about his wife.

"Nothing could stop me remembering my wife that night of May 21. . . . As I walked on deck I believed I could see her in the water beckoning to me. . . . So certain was I that I got two lifebelts, lashed them together, and dived into the sea. I quickly surfaced and began to search for my wife. The water was ice cold and I saw the lights of the ship disappearing."

Mr Ellis said that with the coming of the dawn and the sun, he thought he was going to die.

Badly sunburned he was about to give up hope of rescue, but he saw one or two ships and waved. They did not see him so he decided to strike out for the shore. He was 100 miles off the coast of Guinea.

Finally, after 10 hours in the water, he was seen and picked up by the Italian tanker Esso Augusta.

The captain was not allowed to put the rescued man ashore at Cape Town so he arranged for him to be transferred to a supply boat at the Gulf port of Dubai where Mr Ellis stepped ashore today.—Reuter.

## Council house ghost wore a coat

A GHOST in a check coat is plaguing a block of council homes.

The ghost first appeared at 23-year-old Mrs. Sandra Walters's at Thames View, Barking, Essex, two years ago.

She claimed it went away after Canon, James Roxburgh. Vicar of Barking, held an exorcism service. But now it is back again.

She said yesterday: "A friend has seen it four times. It's a man and wears a check coat. He's always heading for my four-year-old son Steven's room.

### VOICES

"We hear voices, doors opening and people walking round at night. I'm petrified. I can't stand it much longer."

Mrs Walters's neighbour, Mrs Jessie Gothard, has also seen the ghost. "Once it threw Steven's bike down the stairs at me," she said. "I had to go to hospital with face injuries."

Both women have asked the council for a move.

Local curate, the Rev David Thompson, believes the ghost may have been conjured up by seances held by previous tenants.

"The trouble is," he said, "if these families move, the new tenants may find themselves entertaining the ghost instead.

"Most people are sceptical about happenings like this, but I'm convinced there are evil spirits in the maisonette."

He said he would be prepared to conduct another exorcism service.

# 1.
# TALKING
# OF GHOSTS

'Talking of ghosts,' Dr Samuel Johnson observed one day to his friend and biographer, James Boswell, 'it is wonderful that six thousand years have now elapsed since the creation of the world, and still it is undecided whether or not there has ever been an instance of the spirit of any person appearing after death. *All argument is against it, but all belief is for it.*'

According to the Oxford English Dictionary a ghost is the spirit or immaterial part of a man as distinct from the body, and is spoken of as appearing in visible form or otherwise manifesting itself to the living. The word itself is derived from the Saxon *gaste* or *gest*, and in the north of England the term 'guest' is still occasionally used to describe an apparition.

We all, of course, have our own ideas about ghosts, their appearance, actions and intentions – and whether they constitute a subject worthy of consideration or should be consigned to the realms of children's story books. Experts who have studied the phenomenon – and such it surely is whether you are believer or not – have established what they consider are five basic explanations for apparitions:

1. That we have lived previous lives ourselves, and ghosts are reincarnations – dressed in the garments of the period – of people half-consciously remembered from this prior existence.

2. That they are the result of great mental conflict which has imprinted a 'photograph on the astral light' which anyone with the slightest glimmer of psychic faculty can perceive.

3. That they are hybrid beings created by the disembodied spirit of a dead person combining with some substance to produce a temporary, though very elementary, intelligence.

4. That they are produced out of the universal fascination and fear of ghosts by static memory and dynamic consciousness – that is, a layer of consciousness superimposed upon a mechanism of memory.

5. That we actually do see ghosts – dead people being able to build up their bodily forms, somewhat unsubstantially of course, and thereby revisit the scenes in which they spent their lives.

It is perhaps not surprising that even such wide-ranging definitions as these fail to satisfy all the 'specifications' of the ghost, but perhaps they underline the basic truth of the great psychic researcher G. N. M. Tyrrell's comment, 'Why are ghosts so fascinating? Because they have always responded to some innate longing in human nature to pierce the veil which hides the future after death.'

Theorizing apart – although we shall be returning to theories at various stages of this survey – ghosts can be variously 'classified' for ease of identification. Firstly there is the ghost which returns to haunt the earth without harm to man, sometimes bringing messages or warnings; the poltergeist, a destructive, noisy, and impish spirit which hurls objects about and makes strange noises; the 'fetch' or double of someone living or about to die; and finally the spectral animal or creature – not to mention the occasional inanimate object such as a phantom ship – which usually haunts lonely wastes.

Ghosts do not, of course, appear to order. Many a researcher or nervous amateur has watched fruitlessly through long night hours waiting for the

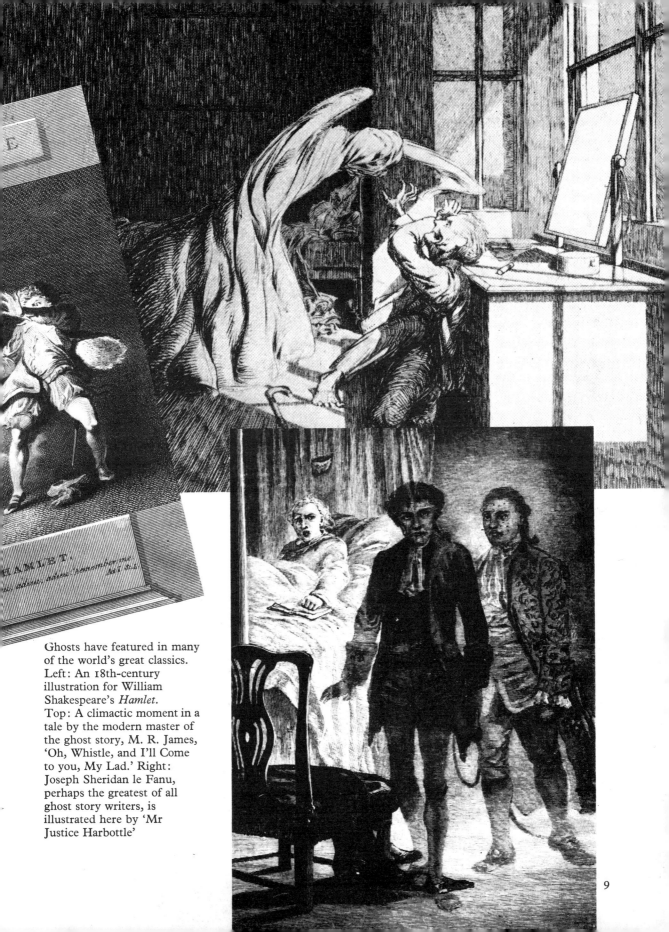

Ghosts have featured in many of the world's great classics. Left: An 18th-century illustration for William Shakespeare's *Hamlet*. Top: A climactic moment in a tale by the modern master of the ghost story, M. R. James, 'Oh, Whistle, and I'll Come to you, My Lad.' Right: Joseph Sheridan le Fanu, perhaps the greatest of all ghost story writers, is illustrated here by 'Mr Justice Harbottle'

Haunted homes have proved of enduring interest to generations of students and laymen alike. In these pictures are some of the most famous British mansions. Top left: 'The White Lady of Rosslyn' is said to haunt Rosslyn Castle and her appearance heralds a disaster or death in the family. Top right: Ham House where many people have reported ghostly phenomena. Middle left: At Linlithgow Palace in Scotland the ghost of Queen Margaret is said to appear on the eve of the Battle of Flodden Field awaiting the return of James IV. Middle right: The haunted crypt of Glamis Castle. Bottom: The house at Burton Agnes where the famous 'screaming skull' resides. Opposite top: Site of John Wesley's poltergeist at Epworth (see p. 52) Bottom: Hampton Court Palace, home of several ghosts (see p. 66)

emergence of a spirit. Moreover, when and if they do come, ghosts are quite likely to be visible to one person in a group and not the rest. Should one confront a ghost though, there is a form of conduct which the late ghost-hunter extraordinary, Harry Price, detailed in his now rare and much-coveted *Blue Book for Psychic Investigations*: 'Do not move, and on no account approach the figure. If the figure speaks, *do not approach*, but ascertain name, age, sex, origin, cause of visit, if in trouble, and possible alleviation. Ask the figure to return, suggesting exact time and place. Do not move until figure disappears. Note exact method of vanishing. If through an open doorway, quietly follow. If through solid object (such as wall) ascertain if still visible on other side.'

However, whether or not you personally see a ghost, for a great many centuries now they have made a lasting impression on humanity, achieving another kind of immortality in whatever form of pictorial representation the man who has seen them has had available. From the clay tablets of the early Babylonians to the parchment drawings of the Romans – from the wooden engravings of the Middle Ages to the magnificent paintings of the seventeenth and eighteenth centuries – and from the hazy glass plates of the Victorian box-camera to the high-speed polaroid of today – all have contributed to the pictorial history of the ghost. And, in a nutshell, what we have done in the pages of this book is to bring together the best of these illustrations. The emphasis all along has been very much on authenticity,

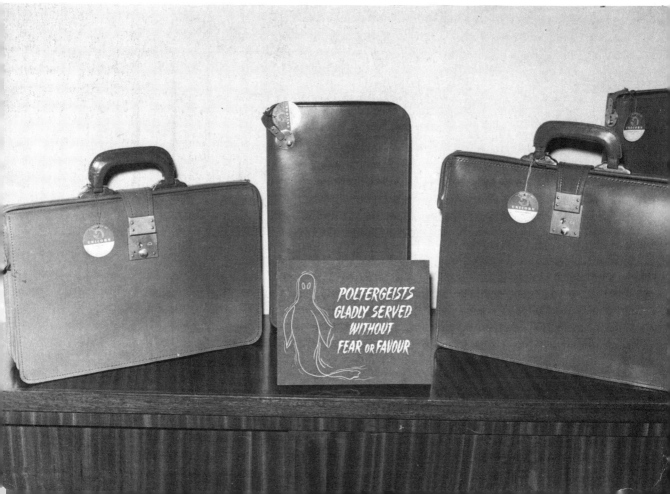

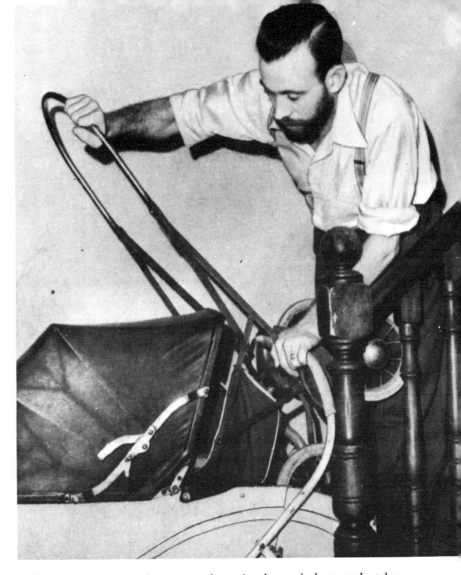

Above: Mr Benson Herbert, a modern ghost hunter, with some of the paraphysical equipment he has designed to investigate scientifically 'things that go bump in the night.' Right: Taking no chances with the troublesome ghost he believes haunts his Plymouth home, Mr William Hampson barricades himself and his family in for the night

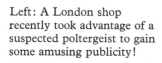

Left: A London shop recently took advantage of a suspected poltergeist to gain some amusing publicity!

with the drawings, paintings, engravings, sketches and photographs taken from the best contemporary sources. Because of this you will not find all the famous ghost stories and hauntings represented – it would be impossible to include the vast number that exist in any one book – but only those which have been most exactly recorded by illustrations made at the time the events occurred. Taken together they constitute a unique history of a subject of perennial interest.

I should perhaps also note that as the ghosts of kings and queens of all periods are in the main so familiar and often so difficult to authenticate, they have not concerned me in these pages. Many other books and papers on this particular aspect of ghost lore have been published and the interested reader is directed to them.

This book does not set out to prove or disprove the actuality of spirits: it merely presents a body of evidence for further discussion. There are some convincing arguments to be encountered, but as with all true mysteries, only the reader can make the final decision for himself. For isn't the best of all evidence that of one's own five senses?

# 2.
# HOMAGE TO THE SPIRITS OF THE DEAD

'A belief in the supernatural has existed in all ages and among all nations' the eminent nineteenth-century ghost-hunter John Netten Radcliffe wrote in his *Fiends, Ghosts and Sprites* (1854) and in those few simple words summed up one of the most enduring of mankind's preoccupations. For ghosts, phantoms, wraiths, spectres, apparitions, poltergeists – manifestations of the supernatural – have always fascinated believer and sceptic alike. Moreover, evidence of this interest is not difficult to find: there can hardly be a household in the country – any country for that matter – which does not boast at least one book on ghost lore; hardly a family that cannot dig up a ghost story recounted by some old relation and still lovingly remembered with a mixture of amusement and a slight sense of unease. In a sentence, belief in ghosts is a subject that has touched everyone, and in these pages we shall try to present the best and most visible evidence of an age-old phenomenon.

The idea of the dead returning in unearthly or spiritual form would seem to date back as far as Stone Age Man, who as we know buried his dead with ceremonies intended to ensure that the deceased's soul rested easily. We can only conjecture to what extent these primitives were beset by phantoms, but some of the earliest written records of mankind – the cuneiform clay tablets – present us with several legends of apparitions which seem already to be of considerable antiquity. On their evidence belief in disembodied spirits can definitely be established among the ancient Semitic people of Babylonia. These people had adopted the beliefs of the primitive Sumerians who dwelt in the valleys of the Euphrates, among whom it was commonly held that the dead visited the earth in spirit form.

Early man believed that these spirits fell into three distinct categories. The first was the disembodied spirit or the soul of the dead. The second was a phantom or demon of terrible appearance whose mission was to harass the living. And, thirdly, there was the peculiar part-human, part-ghost spirit, which was the offspring of intermarriage between human beings and the denizens of the spirit world.

The Assyrians were among the earliest peoples to carefully define the different spirits, and names for several, primarily of an evil nature, appear in their records. There was the *utukku*, a ghost which lay in wait for unsuspecting passers-by in deserted countryside or graveyards and could inflict serious illness on all who merely saw it. Similarly the *alu* – a terrifying spectre which sometimes appeared without a mouth, sometimes without ears or limbs, sprang on the unwary and 'enveloped them as in a garment', to quote one contemporary record. The *alu* occasionally pursued a man into his own dwelling; but the spectre most closely associated with the home was the *ekimmu*, the spirit of an unburied body, whose appearance was said to presage a death in the family. This restless spirit was sometimes heard to 'gibber and cry', and here we have the origin of the tradition of the banshee and other visitants who come 'calling and bringing news of death or disaster'. The Assyrians believed that all these spirits were the direct result of either failure to offer due rites to the dead or leaving a corpse unburied.

Previous page: The temptation of St Anthony by a beautiful spectre. Or was it an L.S.D. hallucination?

An ancient papyrus
illustration of an Egyptian
ghost, or *khu*, on its journey
to judgement at the
'Tribunal of Osiris'

Specific descriptions of the earliest known apparitions are not plentiful, but the Babylonians have left us a most dramatic story in the form of the *Epic of Gilgamish* which, over 4,000 years old, may well be the oldest of all ghost stories. The tale concerns a Babylonian hero, Gilgamish, who appeals to the god Negral to restore his friend and is rewarded by an apparition that rises up like wind in the form of a transparent human shape.

The ancient Egyptians had perhaps the most extensive canon of demons and spirits, the majority of whom prowled about the land seeking to harm humanity unless propitiated. According to Sir Ernest Wallis Budge, the Egyptologist, the peculiar ideas which the Egyptians held about man's constitution influenced their belief in ghosts. They felt that a man consisted of a physical body, a spiritual body, a shadow, a soul, a heart, a spirit called *khu*, a power and a name. The *khu*, unlike the other ephemeral aspects of the person, became at death a wandering and unhappy spirit, which apart from causing illness to the living could also possess the bodies of animals, driving them into a frenzy. The *khu* of suicides, executed criminals, those drowned at sea and the unburied dead were believed to be the most malevolent and the source of much torment.

Apart from appeasing the ghosts by ritual offerings, the Egyptians believed they could communicate with the spirits of the departed, and one famous ancient papyrus in the Cairo Museum records the conversation that a priest, Khonsu-em-heb, held with a spirit which recounted details of his life and future to him. Sometimes in an effort to placate a particularly troublesome spirit, a scroll appealing to the dead man would be placed on his tomb; in this the subject of the haunting would repeat that he had done nothing to deserve this torment and that when both met at the 'Tribunal of Osiris' he would be proved to have right on his side and immediately qualify for the delights of the afterworld.

The Arabs, who also believed in many kinds of ghosts, held that if a man were murdered, his *afrit* or spectre would rise from the ground where the blood had been shed, unless it could be restrained by driving a new nail into the ground where the outrage had been committed. This tradition, known as 'nailing down the ghost', has a very definite affinity with the vampire legend and the method for rendering it harmless.

As one ranges through the histories of other nations at this very early period, one finds how similar the ghost traditions are – in particular that still prevailing idea about ruined buildings being invariably haunted. Authorities are agreed that this stemmed from the belief that while ghosts would obviously prefer occupied buildings these were more often than not protected against intrusion by amulets and charms, and they therefore had to seek refuge where no such obstructions existed. It is also interesting to find that the tradition of a ghost's being able to make a person's hair stand on end with fright is of the very earliest date. An Assyrian text of about 2000 B.C. comments on a man who has just seen a ghost:

> He – the hair of whose body an evil
> Fiend hath set on end.

Similarly the flesh was said to creep unless prayers were uttered immediately, and stories of exorcism or 'laying ghosts' by ritual and the burning of candles and incense date back to the Babylonians and beyond. In all these early stories, too, accounts of ghosts describe them as being of human shape and visage; so if, as sceptics would have it, we are fooled by tales of ghosts today, mankind has been fooled in just the same way for much of recorded time!

It is with the Greeks and Romans that we find the first really detailed descriptions of ghosts and their mythology. Both believed that the souls of the dead, called *manes*, wandered about the earth to haunt the wicked, terrify the good and generally interfere in the affairs of the living. The spirits of those who had led virtuous lives were distinguished by the name of *lares*; those of the wicked were termed *larvae* or *lemures*, and just as often terrified the good as the impious. These ghosts were also deified, being referred to as *dii manes*, and the stones erected over graves in Roman burial grounds were usually inscribed with the letters D.M. or D.M.S., meaning *Dis Manibus* or *Dis Manibus Sacrum*, 'Sacred to the Manes Gods'. Sacrifices were offered to these deities, the offerings being termed *religiosae*, as distinct from the *sacrae* offered to the superior gods. And during the festivals in honour of the *lemuria*, it was customary to burn black beans over the graves and to beat drums, so that the noxious fumes of the first and the noise of the second would drive away any ghosts in the vicinity.

Some of the best examples of the Greek conception of apparitions are to be found in the pages of the *Odyssey*, which was probably written around 630 B.C. During his voyages, Ulysses has several encounters with ghosts, but no passage is I think more representative of both the book and the

current social attitude to such phenomena than this:

Thus solemn rites and holy vows we paid
To all the phantom nations of the dead.
There died the sheep; a purple torrent flow'd,
And all the caverns smoked with streaming blood,
When lo! appear'd along the dusky coasts,
Thin airy shoals of visionary ghosts;
Fair pensive youths, and soft enamour'd maids
And wither'd elders, pale and wrinkled shades;
Ghastly with wounds, the forms of warriors slain
Stalked with majestic port, a martial train.
These and a thousand more swarm'd o'er the ground,
And all the dire Assembly shriek'd around.
Astonished at the sight, aghast I stood
And a cold fear ran shivering through my blood.

In the *Aeneid* we are given a description of a ghost whose timeless quality makes it almost like a modern ghost story:

'Twas in the dead of night, when sleep repairs
Our bodies worn with toils, our minds with cares,
When Hector's ghost before my sight appears:
A bloody shroud he seem'd, and bath'd in tears.

Virgil also informs us that the Greeks believed that Charon was not permitted to ferry the ghosts of unburied persons over the Styx, and so they wandered up and down the banks for hundreds of years, after which they were finally permitted to cross.

The satirist Lucian brought a little light relief to the subject by writing of a 'ghost club' whose members met in order to discuss apparitions and other phenomena, in a manner which we would now describe as 'psychic research'!

Roman history is similarly replete with tales of apparitions, and a fascinating occurrence is recorded by Pliny, the consul at Sura. There was a house at Athens haunted by a ghost who roamed through the building at night, apparently dragging a heavy chain behind him. Athenodorous, the philosopher, hired the house and determined to quiet the spirit. One night, while he was pursuing his studies, the silence was broken by the rattling of chains, and presently the spectre entered the room. At first Athenodorous (brave man!) took no notice, but then the chains began to rattle again and when he did look up the ghost beckoned to him to follow. He was led out into the courtyard by his ghostly guide who pointed to a certain spot on the ground – and then promptly vanished. Much puzzled, the philosopher marked the place and next day had the ground dug up. There the skeleton of a man in chains was found; Athenodorous had it publicly burned and thereafter the ghost was seen no more.

The story of Caesar's violent end, foretold to his wife Calpurnia by a ghostly spirit, is too well-known to need more than passing mention here, just as is the legend that the Emperor's ghost returned to haunt his assassin, Brutus. But this was not the only time that the unfortunate Brutus was

Above: The spectre of Julius Caesar appearing to Brutus

Left: Ulysses' encounter with ghosts – an early illustration from the *Odyssey*

Left: King Belshazzar at a drunken feast sees a hand writing of doom to come on the wall of his palace

Below: Ghosts took on many forms in Japanese legend – here the famous hunter Aki-no-Kami encounters the apparition of the fox goddess Koki-teno

'visited': another spectre, this time predicting his death, appeared to him when his army and that of Cassius were waiting to do battle with the triumvirate in Greece. One night, according to a record of the incident, Brutus was in his tent working when he saw at his side a ghost that was 'horrifying in its gigantic proportions and pale, emaciated face'. For a time the spectre remained silent, but then Brutus spoke: 'Who are you, Man or God? Tell me. What do you want?' At which the spectre replied, 'I am your evil spirit. You will see me again at Philippi.' And, 'the phantom did indeed reappear to Brutus on the night preceding his defeat and death.'

Northern Europe at this time also abounded in legends of ghosts, and it was customary with the Scandinavians as with other peoples to perform ceremonies at the tombs of the dead to propitiate ghosts and facilitate their entrance into the 'halls of bliss'. To see examples of this, one has only to turn to the early Scandinavian traditions and historical writings such as the legend of Helge and Sigrun and the Eyrbyggja Saga, which describes the apparitions plaguing the family of an Icelandic woman whose death-bed commands had not been obeyed.

Similarly in India, there were the fearsome ghosts known variously as *virikas*, *paisachi* or *bauta*, the latter being particularly horrendous with small red bodies, the teeth of lions and the habit of roaming abroad at night gibbering in a nasal tone. It was customary in many parts of the country to erect small shrines to them, formed of a pile of stones on top of which was a sheltered cavity containing an image to which food and other offerings were presented from time to time. Already at this time there was in the country a class of men called *cani* or *shaycana*, who were supposed to have the power of frightening away troublesome spirits, and who charged a fee depending on the alleged powers of the ghost and its relationship to the family concerned.

The Chinese were another race who dreaded ghosts, particularly of those

Right: The apparition of a flying head, a famous American Indian legend, depicted in a 19th-century engraving

who had been murdered. According to legend, the Chinese spirit is first seen in shapeless form, the head forming first, then the feet, and finally the body. The faces are said to have no chins. Chinese customs and classic literature (for example the ancient plays) are full of references to apparitions, seen in the clothes they wore on earth and surrounded by a green light. There is in Chinese records a list of sixty '*Shin* of Offence', or evil ghosts, each of which appeared for one day during a cycle of sixty days. To drive off these spectres, the people hung on their walls certain talismans of iron decorated with perforated money and pictures of warriors. They also propitiated them with a curious ceremony called 'Appeasing the Burning Mouths' which took place on the seventeenth day of the seventh moon, when plates of cakes were laid out bearing invitations addressed to the 'Honourable Homeless Ghosts'.

A rich and long-enduring tradition also exists in Japan, where ghosts are said to appear in innumerable forms. Among the most frequent are the apparitions of women with dishevelled hair, clad in white flowing robes, and warriors carrying Samurai swords. Almost invariably these phantoms are shown without legs and bearing scars appropriate to their earthly misdeeds; they are not usually malevolent, but can exercise a perverse and wicked ingenuity. Ghosts in Japan are also said to take the form of foxes which change into beautiful women and bewitch all who cross their paths.

The North-American Indians have also revered spirits since time immemorial, and their 'Ghost Dance' in honour of the dead is one of the most colourful and exciting ceremonies in the world. These first American ghosts were noisy beings: there is a saying among the Algonquin Indians that 'the shadow souls of the dead chirp like crickets.'

Belief in ghosts features quite extensively in the evolution of Christianity, as the theologian Dr Robert Watts points out. 'The Scriptures,' he writes, 'make mention of ghosts thus: Matthew 14:26, when the Disciples saw Jesus walking on the water, "they thought it had been a spirit"; and Luke 24: 37, "after His resurrection they saw Him at once appearing in the midst of them, and they supposed they had seen a spirit." And our Saviour does not contradict their notion, but argues with them upon the supposition of its truth, "A spirit hath not flesh and bones, as ye see me to have."' The Christian fathers make similar references in their writings. Evodius, the friend of St Augustine and Bishop of Upsal in Africa, wrote in one of his commentaries that 'I remember well that Profuturus, Privatus and Servitius, whom I had known in the monastery here, appeared to me and talked to me after their decease and what they told me happened.' The venerable old man believed that the soul, after quitting the body, retained a 'certain subtle shape not unlike its human form' in which it appeared and was transported from one place to another. He left several reports given to him by others of ghosts seen moving about in houses, and also of nocturnal visitants to churches who were heard praying aloud. Evodius, like St Augustine, was not an unqualified believer and went to some pains to distinguish between what he considered were real ghosts and the 'false visions of disordered minds'.

Erasmus, in one of his epistles, tells the story of a fake ghost which appeared to a 'rich woman, well monied and withall very covetous'. Unfortunately the man's attempt to scare the lady to death by covering himself with a white sheet and making 'certaine rumblings and noyses in the ayre' went wrong when she took a stick to the 'apparition' and beat it until it cried out for mercy!

Perhaps the most famous ghost story in the Bible features in 1 Samuel 28, when King Saul, alarmed at the likely outcome of his battle with the Philistine army, summoned a necromancer to raise the spirit of his predecessor, Samuel, for advice. There has been much theological debate as to whether the necromancer – a woman referred to as the Witch of Endor – actually summoned a ghost or whether she used some form of optical illusion combined with ventriloquism to create the figure which warned Saul of forthcoming doom. Whatever the case, the story does illustrate the place of spirits in Biblical history.

The famous Christian ascetic, St Anthony, who lived much of his life in abstinence and devotion and is regarded as the founder of Christian monasticism, allegedly had numerous encounters with demons and ghosts. Doubtless, St Anthony's extensive fasting may have been in part responsible for both the apparitions and the 'filthy and maddening thoughts' which plagued him. It has been suggested recently that he may have eaten bread infected with the fungus *Claviceps purpurea*, which contains lysergic acid, the natural source of L.S.D. – and that this would account for many of his 'visions'; nonetheless, his struggles with phantoms have provided a rich source of inspiration for painters, several of whom have given much attention to the beautiful female ghost which allegedly attempted to lure him into carnal pleasures.

To this very day Christianity has, of course, continued to acknowledge the possibility of ghosts and spirits, and indeed the service of exorcism is still employed for driving out harmful spirits and for combating devils.

Above: Another of the early
Christian Fathers who
experienced visions and
ghostly phenomena was St
Augustine. This picture by
Garofalo is in the National
Gallery, London

Right: The dramatic
encounter of King Saul with
a phantom raised by the
Witch of Endor

# 3.
# POLTERGEISTS
# AND MAGICIANS

The dark span of human history stretching from the fall of the Roman Empire to Columbus's discovery of America in the sixteenth century brought a general consolidation of the belief in ghosts and apparitions: many of the superstitions and legends about phantoms which had already evolved in earlier times were now given still wider credence, and this, coupled with the enormous extent to which the occult sciences were practised during the period, gave rise to the widespread feeling that supernatural factors exercised an especially great influence over the affairs of man. Such indeed was the prevalence of these beliefs that there was hardly a local or national event which did not seem pregnant with mystery. Legends proliferated, all drawing on the traditional figures of giants, witches, wizards, demons and ghosts – some of which were to form the basis of the famous nursery and children's stories, such as 'Jack the Giant Killer', 'Puss in Boots' and 'Cinderella'. The countryside, too, was strange and mysterious; the castles of the nobility were dank and forbidding, the hovels of the peasants wretched and evil-smelling. There was little light to fall on any of this darkness, and small wonder that each shadow and movement took on a life of its own. Ghosts of the dead lurked by every castle wall, phantom horsemen galloped crazily through every village and evil spectres glided around every human habitation.

The crusades in the thirteenth century provided the setting of one of the earliest well-documented ghost stories of the period, the main details of which are to be found in Matthew Paris's *English History* (1259). The story concerns an English nobleman, William Longespee or Longsword, who was brutally hacked to death while fighting the Saracens in a battle along the Nile in 1250. At the moment of his death, it is said, an apparition of the knight appeared to his mother, the Abbess of Lacock in England. The figure was little more than a skeleton, but the Abbess recognized her son by the insignia on his shield, and started back in horror when the spirit said, 'It is your son, William, and I have been brought down to honour God's name.' The Abbess later reported her visitation to others, but no one was prepared to believe her until finally, six months later, a messenger arrived from Egypt bringing confirmation of William Longespee's sad end.

Another authenticated ghost story of this time concerns the beautiful Château Blandy, situated a few miles from Melun on the plains of Briand in France. A contemporary chronicler outlining the facts of this story felt compelled to warn his readers that 'We shall be alarmed by the frequent apparitions of the Château of Blandy; we shall read with a thrill of horror of the mysterious noises which are heard on every winter night, in the dark turrets of the old chateau.' According to history, several bloody murders and tragedies had been enacted within the grounds of the castle, one of the worst of these involving a steward who had stolen some of the family jewels; in attempting to hide them in an old hollow tree he had fallen into it, and was trapped there undiscovered until after his death.

His ghost then joined those of previous tenants of the castle, who at midnight on the day of All Saints were said to be seen floating in the air, circling around the edifice until finally coming to rest on a tower near the

Previous page: The Elizabethan occultist Dr John Dee and his companion Edward Kelly raising the spirit of a dead man at Walton-le-Dale in Lancashire

Right: The phantom crusader – an illustration of Matthew Paris's story of the ghost of the English nobleman, William Longespee

Below: An old print of the Blandy Castle apparition in Briand, France

entrance. On that night too the sound of clanking chains together with piercing shrieks and cries could be heard rising from the depths of a secret subterranean passage which no one had the courage to explore. The most famous of this band of apparitions was said to be that of Count Dunois, a previous owner, who on one night of every year was also seen standing by himself at the gate of the château armed from head to foot and accompanied by an escort all clad in armour. It was believed that on these occasions 'the blasts of the war clarions were heard, together with the clash of weapons and the tumult of a moving army.'

The ancient German castle of Rosenberg-Neuhaus also had an apparition, a 'White Lady' who was first seen during the fifteenth century. The spirit was said to be that of Perchta von Rosenberg, born about 1420 and the wife of John von Lichtenstein, a rich and profligate baron, who made her life so wretched that she eventually died of 'the insults and indescribable distress she endured'. Thereafter the corridors of the castle became the haunt of, a tall figure in white 'wearing a widow's veil adorned with ribbons, through the folds of which a faint light was said to glimmer'. In later years the spirit was said to appear when a death was about to occur in the family, and at times she visited the castles of other families called Rosenberg at Brandenburg, Baden and Darmstadt. She also made a famous appearance in Berlin in 1628 when she exclaimed to a descendant, 'Come, judge the living and the dead; my fate is not yet decided.'

It is in the Dark Ages that we find the first specific reports of that noisy and troublesome associate of the ghost, the poltergeist. The word poltergeist is an old German folk-lore term meaning literally a spirit (*geist*) that causes a noise or uproar (*polter*). Its activities – moving objects, flinging stones and earth about, creating noises such as raps, bangs, scratchings, and even occasionally human sounds such as whistling, singing and talking – no doubt gave rise to that classic phrase about 'things that go bump in the night'. One of the earliest recorded occurrences of a poltergeist did in fact take place in Germany, at Bingen-am-Rhein, where in the year 355 people were pulled out of bed, stones were thrown, and terrific raps and blows were heard throughout the village. The same locality was visited again in 856 when showers of stones and thunderous noises occurred in Kembden near Bingen. This time an ethereal voice was heard accusing a priest of conducting an intrigue, and revealing the secret misdeeds of a number of villagers. The possessions of the principal offender of this group were simultaneously destroyed by fire!

Italy, too, seems to have suffered at an early date from the activities of these spirits, and there are several stories of showers of stones being hurled at people in the years between 534 and 562.

In Britain, the great chronicler, Giraldus Cambrensis, refers to a case in Pembroke in the twelfth century where mud was flung about, holes were ripped in garments and a spirit conversed in an angry voice with two people, Stephen Wiriet and William Not. Giraldus also tells us that exorcism was tried but proved ineffective, the priests themselves being attacked. A little later, during the reign of Richard I, a 'visual and tactile poltergeist phenomenon' was recorded in the home of Sir Osborne of

Above: A contemporary woodcut of the visionary portents seen in the sky over Germany in 1507

Top: A phantom army seen over Lyons in 1557 and recorded in the *Prodigiorum Chronicon*

Right: The ghost of a drowned traveller appearing to his wife in a 15th-century German engraving

Of ghoſtes
and ſpirites walking
by nyght,
and of ſtrange noyſes, crackes, and
ſundry forewarnynges, whiche
commonly happen before
the death of menne,
great ſlaughters,
& alterations
of kyng-
domes.
One Booke,
Written by Lewes Laua-
terus of Tigurine.
And tranſlated into Eng-
lyſhe by R. H.

London by Henry Benneyman
d VVatkyns. 1572.

Left: 'The White Lady', Perchta von Rosenberg, appearing in the 15th century

Bottom left: Cover of the first book in English to describe the poltergeist phenomena

Below: A German illustration of the 'Fetches', or spirit doubles, of people still alive

Right: A spectre accosting Charles VI ('Charles the Foolish') in the Forest of Mans in 1392

Bradaewelle, at Dagworth in Suffolk. This apparition spoke to a number of people, sometimes revealing the 'secret doings of others'; it remained in residence for some time.

In the fourteenth-century we find several recorded instances in France – one at Alais, near Avignon, concerning 'the greislie Gaist of Gye', becoming famous throughout Europe. Here the stories of inexplicable noises, stones being hurled and people buffeted by unseen forces, were made the subject of a papal enquiry, but no explanation could be offered. Jean Bodin in his *Demonomanie des Sorciers* lists several other cases, one of which involved an eighteen-year-old nun who on several occasions was lifted into the air and 'much ill-used by the spirit'.

Left: A beautiful French
engraving of a medieval ghost
said to appear to hunters in
the Alps Maritime

Above: A French portrait of
a ghost which haunted a
mansion in Gascony in the
15th century

A further interesting case was recorded in Europe in 1533 when a group of Franciscan monks investigated the strange scratching and rapping sounds coming from the bed in which a small child slept. The bishop in charge of the enquiry became convinced that the occurrence was a hoax and demanded that the child be punished. As we shall see, children feature quite often in later accounts of poltergeists, frequently being blamed for their activities; however, most contemporary reports of these early poltergeist outbreaks still have a tendency to attribute them to the machinations of witches. For example, Nathaniel Crouch in *The Kingdom of Darkness* (1688) writes: 'And as there are witches, so they are many times the causes of those strange disturbances which are in houses haunted by evil spirits.' As we shall see when we encounter poltergeists again from the seventeenth century onwards, it was not until the erosion of belief in witchcraft as represented by the Inquisition *et al* that accounts of such phenomena were divorced from preconception, separately recorded and individually evaluated.

As I mentioned earlier, the occult sciences were widely studied during the Middle Ages, and magicians and alchemists flourished throughout Britain and Europe. These men, poring over their ancient books of forbidden lore, sought the secret of life and the ability to transmute metals into gold, as well as making contact with the spirits of the dead. Their experiments were usually dangerous, not infrequently fatal, and consequently they were held in awe if not actually feared by much of the population. Later occultists have for generations been studying the lives of these men for whom the most grandiose of claims were made. Reports of their finding the elixir of life, of creating the *homoclus* and of raising the dead, proliferated in the Middle Ages – as did wild rumours about the secrets contained in their forbidden manuals. That they sought to raise spirits and pry into the nature of ghosts is undisputed; it is the varied reports of their success which now need the expert's most careful scrutiny.

French occultists were particularly active in this area, and came to believe that when a corpse was buried the salts it contained were given off during the heating process of fermentation. The saline particles then resumed the same relative positions that they had occupied in the living body, and a complete human form was reproduced. This was the reason, they argued, that ghosts habitually frequented graveyards; and in an attempt to duplicate the process, they performed many experiments with blood, from which it was believed that the saline particles emanated. One such experimenter was a Frenchman, Joseph La Pierre, who spent a whole week applying various degrees of fire to samples of blood he had obtained. A report of his work by the Lord of Bourdalone in 1482 tells us:

> About midnight, the Friday following, when lying betwixt sleeping and waking, he heard a terrible noise like the roaring of a lion. And continuing quiet after the sound had ceased, the moon being at the full, suddenly betwixt himself and the window he saw a thick little cloud, condensed into an oval form which after, little by little, did seem completely to put on the shape of a woman and making

33

another and sharp clamour, did suddenly vanish.

But the occultist said that in this he found solace, because the bishop of whom he had the blood did admonish him, that if any of them from whom the blood was extracted should die in the time of its putrefaction, his spirit was wont often to appear to the sight of the operator with perturbation.

Occultist Thomas Perks raising demons and ghosts with the aid of a medieval grimoire

Shortly afterwards, three German occultists who had tried a variation of this formula by distilling earth collected from a graveyard claimed that they had seen 'the spirits of men' in their glass vessels.

Perhaps the best documented account of one of these *Magii* is that of John Dee (1527–1608), who despite his achievements as a philosopher and scholar is more widely remembered as 'a companion of hellhounds and a conjuror of wicked and damned spirits'. Much of his early life was devoted to travelling in Europe, where he amassed a formidable library of books on witchcraft and the raising of spirits, and met several famous contemporary demonologists, including Johan Weyer and Jean Bodin. Returning to England, he spent a great deal of time deciphering his literary collection, casting horoscopes and enquiring deeply into black and white magic. At this period he also confessed to having strange dreams, and began an investigation into spirits and visions which was to occupy him for much of the rest of his life. He believed it was possible to make contact with what he called 'angels', and indeed compiled several manuscripts of conversations with these 'ethereal beings' which are now pre-

Joseph La Pierre, the French occultist, who allegedly created ghosts from human blood

served in the British Museum. (Because of this work, Dee is regarded by several modern authorities as one of the pioneers of Spiritualism)

The event which was to make him most famous – though it undoubtedly obscured many of his more notable achievements – was an experiment he conducted with his erstwhile partner, John Kelly, a rogue and confidence trickster. This took place in the churchyard at Walton-le-dale in Lancashire where they used magical incantations to raise the spirit of a dead man and converse with it. The illustration of this bizarre event is now one of the most famous pictures in occult history.

Whether they did see what is depicted – or whether it was another of Kelly's frauds (he more than once convinced Dee that it was possible to see ghosts in a special crystal ball of his) – it is now impossible to say. No doubt the activities of Dee and his fellow occultists, characterized by an almost total lack of corroborative evidence, helped to stimulate the first growth of scepticism among educated people at the close of the sixteenth century. Certainly by 1584 the climate of opinion had sufficiently changed for an erudite authority such as Reginald Scot – one of the first writers to question the bigotry and prejudice that surrounded witchcraft – to write: 'Where are the soules that swarmed in time past? Where are the spirits? Who heareth their noises? Who seeth their visions?' But if he, and others, thought that ghosts and apparitions were now disappearing from the stage of human affairs, they were sadly mistaken. For the seventeenth century was to prove one of the busiest of all times for hauntings . . .

# 4.
# PHANTOM DRUMMERS AND GHOSTLY WARNINGS

'If the ghost stories of the seventeenth century had all been recorded and collected, they would have filled hundreds of volumes, for nearly every castle, ruined building and country lane had its traditions of apparitions and uncanny happenings. So wrote one of this century's most dedicated students of the occult, C. J. S. Thompson, in an essay on ghosts published in 1930. 'If they did not make themselves visible in diaphanous forms or audible by moans and groans,' he goes on, 'they rattled chains or made weird noises, and were even said to reveal secret places where treasures were concealed and sometimes to bring crimes to light.' Obviously in a survey such as this it is only possible to cover a small number of these instances, so I have tried to concentrate on the most fascinating cases, those which illustrate the variety of reports, and – naturally – those which are best represented by contemporary engravings.

The case of the Drummer of Tedworth, probably the most famous of this century, has been referred to as 'one of the earliest well-attested poltergeist cases in England'. It took place in the small country district of Tedworth in Wiltshire when there was a sudden outbreak of drumming sounds in the house of the local magistrate, Mr John Mompesson. Children were lifted into the air, shoes were flung at a man's head, chamber-pots were emptied on to beds and a horse had one of its rear legs forced into its mouth. Mompesson, a sober, conscientious and well-respected man, was just one of many witnesses to these phenomena which first occurred in the spring of 1662 and continued for exactly a year. The events began in March when an itinerant conjuror and one-time regimental drummer, William Drury, was arrested for obtaining money with forged documents. He was brought before Magistrate Mompesson, who decided to let him off with a warning, but confiscated his drum and told him to leave the district. Almost immediately afterwards the drumming sounds commenced; witnesses reported seeing the drum rise in the air inside Mr Mompesson's house and give off booming sounds. After several nights of this the sleepless Magistrate had it broken up; but the following night the sounds continued unabated, this time above the house, and the other strange manifestations also began to be seen. Those who naturally suspected that the vagrant Drury had secretly returned and was to blame were soon proved wrong, for the man had been arrested for theft in Gloucester and sentenced to transportation. Stories of the Drummer soon spread throughout the country, and one of the first people to come to investigate was the famous Reverend Joseph Glanville, chaplain to Charles II and author of the famous witchcraft study, *Saducismus Triumphatus*. He heard the drumming 'usually five nights together . . . on the outside of the house which is most of it board' and collected eye-witness accounts from children and servants. A committee subsequently appointed by the King to enquire into the case heard nothing, and could deduce no human agency.

As a result of his work Glanville might well be regarded as the father of modern psychical research; certainly we have him to thank for the detailed nature of the report of this strange case, and for the location of similar accounts of drums being beaten and rifles shot at several places in Yorkshire and Lincolnshire a little earlier in 1658; these however only served to

Previous page: An amusing comment on the famous 'Phantom Drummer of Tedworth' by George Cruikshank

38

Right: Contemporary engraving of the 'Phantom Drummer of Tedworth' over Mr Mompesson's house. From Joseph Glanville's *Saducismus Triumphatus*

Below: Cotton Mather who studied and recorded poltergeist phenomena in America

heighten the mystery of the Drummer of Tedworth.

Glanville was also responsible for the formation of a group of people who met at Ragley Hall in Warwickshire to read and discuss reports on contemporary haunted houses, ghosts, apparitions and poltergeists, and most interestingly of all, test those who said they could contact spirits. No doubt it was their activities which, as Harry Price, the modern ghost-hunter, puts it, 'first stimulated those persons fortunate enough to possess a ghost, to investigate the affair in a proper manner, to record the case systematically, and to have the phenomenon attested by responsible witnesses.'

In America, too, at this time, poltergeists had made their presence felt. Cotton Mather, the fervent Puritan and witchcraft-prosecutor, recorded instances in 1662 of stones being thrown at people and windows at the home of a Mr George Walton in Plymouth. Mather was unable to offer any explanation of the events – he did not even try to ascribe them to witchcraft, his favourite scapegoat – but made a great point of the fact that the stones only hit people gently! Cotton Mather's father, Increase Mather, also recorded an alleged instance of a poltergeist at Brightling in 1659, but this proved to be a fraud which was detected by the local minister, Reverend Joseph Bennett. Nevertheless Increase was a believer in such phenomena and wrote about the Drummer of Tedworth among others in his book *Remarkable Providences* (1684). He was also a friend and correspondent of the Reverend Joseph Glanville in England.

Another well-known English ghost legend originally from this period concerns Herne the Hunter, the phantom huntsman said to gallop wildly through Windsor Forest. It has proved impossible to determine precisely when the story first arose – some authorities believe it may even be medieval – but the weight of evidence suggests that the ghost first appeared in the seventeenth century and was that of a forest keeper named Herne, who, accused of a crime, hanged himself on an oak tree in order to escape justice. Thereafter his ghost was seen in the vicinity of the tree or galloping through the forest. According to tradition he was a malignant phantom with staring eyes and stag-like horns, and all those who saw his face were doomed to illness and disaster. On the basis of this scant information, a legend grew up which has fascinated mankind ever since: Shakespeare himself makes use of it in *The Merry Wives of Windsor*.

Many alternative theories have been advanced about the origin of this ghost, the most popular being (a) that he was a poacher, and (b) that he was the leader of a witchcraft coven: hence the 'devil horns' on his head. Accounts of his visitations have continued to the present day, and cattle diseases in the district are often put down to his malice. The most recent reports suggest that he has become a little reluctant to show himself to people, but many still claim to have heard his hunting horn and the sound of his horse's hooves thudding across the common at Cookham Dean near Maidenhead. (Another modern addition to the legend has it that his appearance presages some national disaster or misfortune in the Royal Family.)

Windsor Castle was the setting for another unearthly event in the seventeenth-century, when an armour-clad figure appeared to give warning of forthcoming death. This was the ghost of the late Duke of Buckingham who presented himself to an officer of the king's wardrobe called Parker, commanding him to tell his son, Sir George Villiers, that, 'if he did not somewhat ingratiate himself to the people, or at least, attempt to abate the malice they had against him, he would be suffered to live but a *short time!*' Twice more the Duke visited the terrified servant, on the last occasion drawing a dagger and saying, 'This will end my son.' Parker relayed to his master all that he had been told; according to legend Sir George was 'much troubled' by what he learned, but took no positive action to mend his callous ways, and six months later was dead at the hands of the assassin Felton. An illustration from a seventeenth-century pamphlet *The Full, True and Particular Account of the Ghost or Apparition of the Late Duke of Buckingham's Father* is reprinted here, and must qualify as one of the earliest truly contemporary pictures of a ghost.

Another pamphlet, still extant, recounts the appearance at a man's bedside of the ghost of Cardinal Wolsey. The good churchman emerged in spirit form on the night of 14 May 1641, to converse with the Archbishop of Canterbury and give him guidance. The title page of this work is also reproduced here.

A contemporary of the Archbishop was the Earl of Strafford whose remarkable ghost is said to have appeared to several people in various places, including Charles I at Daventry and Archbishop Laud in the Tower

Above: Herne the Hunter races through Windsor Forest, an engraving by Cruikshank

Below: Shakespeare utilized several true ghost stories in his plays – this is an old illustration of Banquo's ghost appearing to Macbeth

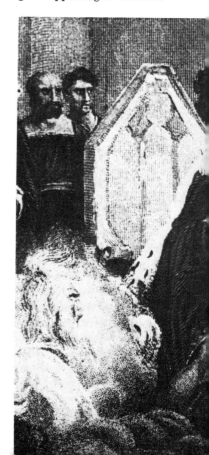

Right: Ghostly intervention
in the lives of the nobility.
Top: The ghost of the Earl
of Stafford from a ballad
sheet of 1641. Middle: A
contemporary pamphlet about
the ghost of Cardinal Wolsey.
Bottom: The ghost of the
Duke of Buckingham gives
dire warning about the future
of his son to a servant

Canterburies
DREAME:
IN WHICH
The Apparition of Cardinall *Wolsey* did
present himselfe unto him on the fourteenth
of May last past:
*It being*
The third night after my Lord of STRAFFORD had
taken his fare-well to the WORLD.

Printed in the yeare 1641.

of London. Visiting the King on the eve of the Battle of Naseby, the spirit warned him not to engage with the parliamentary forces as defeat was inevitable. But after taking advice Charles decided not to heed such a 'quaint' warning – and thereafter suffered his famous and disastrous defeat. In the case of Archbishop Laud, the Earl came to reprove him for his evil ways and to describe the bloody spectacle his head would soon be when 'on London Bridge 'tis raised'. The woodcut of the Earl's ghost shown here is taken from a ballad sheet published in 1641.

It is worth noting the tremendous boost given to superstitious belief by the Civil War in England. The tendency towards melancholy of Cromwell's rigid Puritans seems to have been much played upon by those Royalist supporters whom they seized. 'During their occupancy of some of the old, family seats, formerly the centre of hospitality and good cheer,' one commentator has written, 'their intolerance to the discarded retainers gave rise to many tales calculated to give them a wholesome horror of their surroundings.' One particularly favoured story – it occurs with many different locations, but is believed to have originated at Foxley in Norfolk in 1602 – concerned the appearance of the devil to a miller. According to an Ashmolean manuscript of the story in the Bodleian Library, 'the miller was going from his watermill to his windmill during a tempest, when he saw a man in black before him. When he called to him desiring him to stay till he might speak to him, he turned into a black dog. Coming back from the mill, the miller again saw the man in black and when he spoke to him he turned into a black boar and then vanished away.'

Although this story may have given the Puritans only a passing fright, something much more terrifying lay in wait for the intruders at the Palace of Woodstock in 1649. This building, formerly a royal residence, was

Below: An engraving of the ghost which appeared to a Norfolk miller in 1602

Right: A satirical cartoon on the alleged poltergeist which so terrified Cromwell's men at Woodstock Palace in 1649

Below: A somewhat fanciful engraving of a priest attempting to exorcise evil spirits in the 18th century

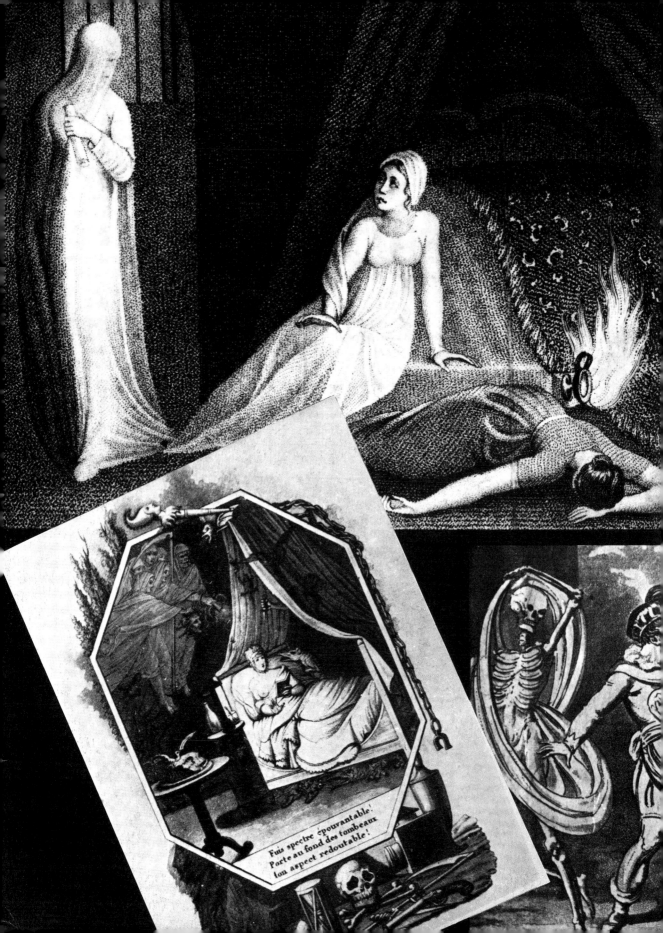

Fuis spectre épouvantable!
Porte au fond des tombeaux
Ton aspect redoutable!

Left: The ghost as it was
popularly represented in
Germany – and much of
Europe – in the 17th century.
Bottom left: A French
engraving of the same period
shows somewhat less
restraint!

Below: The two horrifying
ghosts which appeared to the
dissolute Cassio Burroughs
during the reign of Charles
II – one representing a girl
he had wronged and the
other signifying his coming
death

Top right: The apparition
of the Duchess of Mazarine,
the mistress of Charles II,
who appeared to Madame de
Beauclour, mistress of
James II, in 1674

Bottom right: The royal
ghost of Vienna much
written of in the 17th
century

visited (on the 13th of October, appropriately) by Cromwell's commissioners, who were determined to remove all signs of the King's occupancy. The new residents enjoyed one night of undisturbed sleep – and then the occurrences began: strange shapes were seen, a phantom dog gnawed at the beds, chairs and tables were thrown into the air, curtains were pulled to and fro, candles were mysteriously extinguished, and great noises boomed through the rooms. The commissioners became terrified – one nearly killed a companion when the man appeared during the night wearing only a shirt, which gave him the appearance of a ghost – and after several days of this they gave up their task and fled the palace 'thinking all the fiends of hell had been let loose upon them', to quote one report. The palace continued to be avoided by the Puritans and was regarded as 'ghost haunted' until after the Restoration, when a local prankster, Joseph 'Funny Joe' Collins, a former clerk at the palace, admitted that he had perpetrated the haunting to drive the commissioners away!

A final seventeenth-century English phantom was the Smithfield Market Ghost, first recorded in 1654; this was the spectre of a local laywer named Mallet, who appeared every Saturday night between nine and twelve o'clock and glided through the market pulling joints of meat off the butchers' stalls. A contemporary report – complete with an illustration showing the spectre equipped for his task with projecting horns and hooks – says that the butchers 'adventured to strike at him with cleavers and chopping knives, but cannot feel anything but aire'. According to this source the ghost of lawyer Mallet also ventured further afield – 'unto Whitechappell and Eastcheape and did even more mischief to the butchers than ever Robin Goodfellow did to Country Hides'.

Europe, of course, was just as full of such stories and superstitions, but it is interesting to find that one of the oldest German ghost traditions about the Broken Mountain was finally exploded at about this time.

For centuries the desolate Hartz Mountains in Germany were regarded as the home of giants and weird spectral figures. The Broken Mountain – the highest of the Hartz peaks, rising to some 3,300 feet above sea level – was said to be the most favoured spot of these spirits, who held a grand meeting there on the summit on the first of May every year. Over the years many people had climbed to the peak and returned with horrifying tales of figures towering among the clouds. Then in the closing years of the century a traveller named Gustav Jordan discovered that the spectres were really an illusion. He suddenly realized that the ghostly figure before him was nothing but his own shadow projected on the clouds by the sun. 'It was verified and found,' a contemporary chronicler wrote, 'that when the rising sun threw his rays over the Broken upon the figure of a man standing opposite to fine, light clouds, floating around or hovering past him, he need only fix his eye steadfastly upon them, and in all probability he would see the spectacle of his own shadow extending to the length of from five to six hundred feet, and the distance of about two miles before him, and moving as he moved.' In a way, it was a pity that such a marvellous legend had to be destroyed; but Jordan's discovery did at least reflect a new spirit of enquiry into supernatural matters.

Right: The Spectre of the Brocken – at the top a 17th-century engraving and, below, a picture published at the time the mystery of these 'ghosts' was finally explained

Below: A contemporary woodcut of the notorious Smithfield Ghost who caused such fear among the London meat porters in 1654!

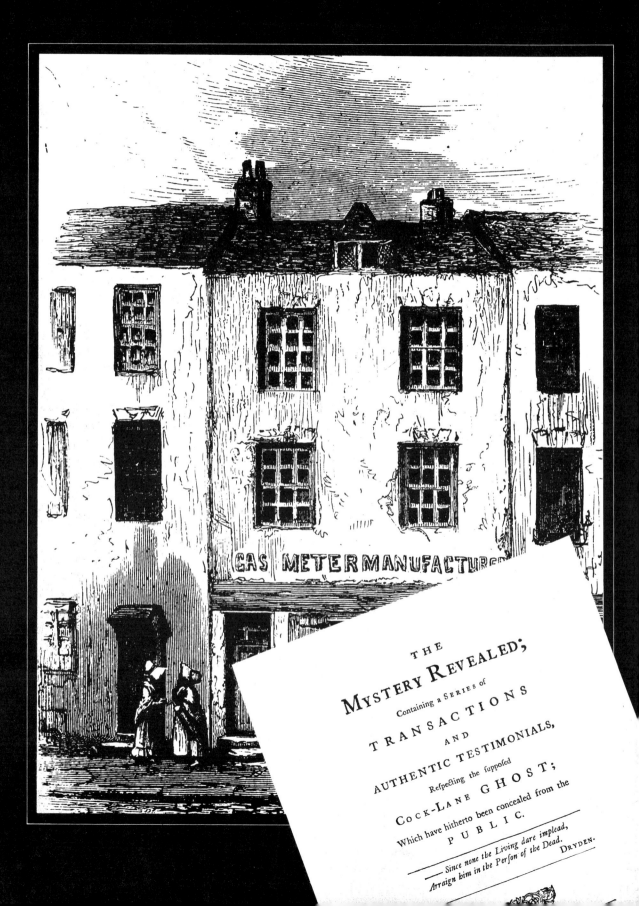

GAS METER MANUFACTURE

THE

MYSTERY REVEALED;

Containing a Series of

TRANSACTIONS

AND

AUTHENTIC TESTIMONIALS,

Respecting the supposed

COCK-LANE GHOST;

Which have hitherto been concealed from the

PUBLIC.

*Since none the Living dare implead,*
*Arraign him in the Person of the Dead.*
DRYDEN.

# 5.
# THE COCK LANE GHOST AND COMMON SENSE

As a result of the tremendous advances made at the beginning of the eighteenth century in the arts and sciences and the general improvement in the human condition, stories of ghosts and apparitions became much discredited. Certainly a great many alleged hauntings were proved to have been faked for personal motives, and many supposedly supernatural ·occurrences dismissed as malicious pranks. As one commentator, James de Loyer, has written, 'Unhappy boys made a special choice of church-yards to terrify others, because they are held to be places most suspected for ghosts and spectres to haunt in and inhabit. In these places they will sometimes set tortoises with burning candles on their backs and let them go, to the intent those that shall see them slowly marching or creeping near the sepulchres.' Yet, for all this scepticism, there were a number of inexplicable occurrences during the century which in time helped to stimulate scientific study of the nature and causes of apparitions.

John Wesley, the renowned preacher, was one man who did not share the public's indifference; he wrote in 1768, 'It is true that the English in general, and indeed most of the men in Europe, have given up all accounts of witches and apparitions as mere old wife's fables. I am sorry for it; giving them up is in effect giving up the Bible.' He had strong personal reasons for his attitude, however, for his family home at Epworth in Lincolnshire, where his father was the minister, had been visited during 1716 and 1717 by a spirit they nicknamed Old Jeffrey. The Epworth Poltergeist, as the ghost became more widely known, was alleged to have disturbed Wesley's young sister Hetty in her bed and to have caused noises and groaning audible throughout the house. Wesley himself was completely convinced of the actuality of the phantom and wrote extensively about it in his *Journal*, thereby giving it an enduring place in ghost history.

Perhaps just as famous as Wesley's poltergeist was the Cock Lane Ghost, which since its appearance in 1762 has attracted the attention of countless investigators and writers. The facts are too well-known to need elaborating here, except to say that the spirit plagued the family of a Mr Richard Parsons in Cock Lane, making rapping and scratching noises and particularly frightening his little daughter Elizabeth, who said she saw 'a shrouded figure without hands'. Dr Samuel Johnson, Horace Walpole, Oliver Goldsmith and the Duke of York visited the house, and huge crowds frequently gathered in the road hoping to hear the mysterious knocking. The phenomenon created a sensation that 'turned all London upside down' according to Andrew Lang in his book *Cock Lane and Common-Sense* (1894). Pamphlets and ballads about the event proliferated, and two of them – one decorated with a bizarre representation of the ghost – are represented here. Opinions about the authenticity of this case have never ceased to fluctuate but having read a great deal of the material myself I am convinced that there is much about it which remains logically inexplicable.

An earlier ghost which had also attracted sightseers was the Guildford Ghost who was 'heard to make his fetters jingle in The White Lion public house in Southwark'. The spirit was that of a Mr Christopher Slaughter-ford of Guildford, who although convicted of murdering his sweetheart

Previous page: The building in Cock Lane which became the centre of public attention after the reports of a poltergeist at work there. The book *The Mystery Revealed* was written by Oliver Goldsmith and was just one of many publications about the strange happenings

Below: A ballad, complete with representation of the ghost, which was sold on the streets of London in 1762

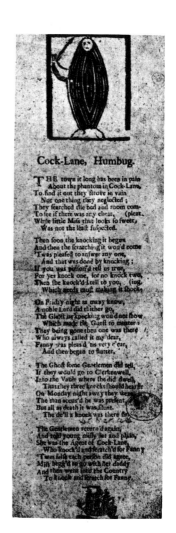

Above: Illustration from the title page of a pamphlet about 'The Guildford Ghost' published in 1709

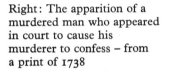

Right: The apparition of a murdered man who appeared in court to cause his murderer to confess – from a print of 1738

Jane Young had protested his innocence as far as the gallows. Slaughterford's ghost later visited both the Marshalsea Prison in Southwark where he had been held during his trial, and the White Lion, where he had stayed briefly after being condemned to death. But the spectre's most amazing appearance took place in Guildford itself, where according to a pamphlet he confronted one of his servants, Joseph Lee, and a friend, Roger Voller, 'in a sad and astonishing manner, in several dreadful and frightful Shapes, with a Rope about his Neck, a flaming torch in one hand and a Club in the Other, crying Vengeance, Vengeance'. Could it be that one of these men was responsible for the murder which Slaughterford had so vehemently denied?

The extraordinary case of a man on trial for murder who saw a ghost in the courtroom also attracted much public interest in 1738. According to the reports, the man had committed a murder which it seemed impossible to prove against him, but when all the witnesses had appeared in the box, he suddenly cried out that he could see 'the murdered person standing upon the step as a witness, ready to be examined against him, and ready to show his throat, which was cut by him (the prisoner)'. So frightened was he, that he confessed to the crime and was swiftly dispatched to the gallows.

Left: A French engraving
of the Headless Ghost who
appeared in the 1760s

Above: The Christian martyr
St Denis who was seen
after his death carrying his
head among those who had
persecuted him

Top right: The ghost which
appeared to a literary man –
from Sir Walter Scott's
*Letters on Demonology and
Witchcraft*

Bottom right: 'The Spectre
of the Oaken Closet', a very
early American illustration
of a ghost which was
reputed to haunt the house
of a New England Puritan
(1780)

Some authenticated cases of that most famous phantom figure, the Headless Ghost, can be found during this period. One location was a small lane at Wortley near Leeds, where a man dressed in a cloak and carrying his head beneath his arm was seen once or twice a year. This spirit was said to be a Yorkshire nobleman who had been executed during the Civil War. A similar report from France, dated 1760, tells of a headless priest who was said to haunt a small village not far from Paris. The man had apparently been a lecher and secret dabbler in witchcraft while he was alive, and a contemporary illustration, reproduced on the previous page, shows two of the young girls he seduced watching his headless form encourage a witch to lure another maiden into the ways of evil. The Christian martyr St Denis is also said to have been seen in ghostly form carrying his head before him and 'creating great fear among those who had so unjustly persecuted him'.

Sir Walter Scott in his *Letters on Demonology and Witchcraft* records the story of an eighteenth-century literary man who was visited by the spectre of an eminent and lately-departed colleague. The man had actually been reading a book by the poet when his ghost appeared, but before he could recover from his shock, the figure slowly vanished into nothingness.

The story of the profligate Lord Thomas Lyttleton and the spectre which appeared to him just before his death is perhaps the last important eighteenth-century English account we need consider. During the night of 24 November 1779, Lord Lyttleton was awoken by what sounded like a bird fluttering by his bed and saw standing before him 'the figure of an unhappy female whom he had seduced and deserted, and who, when deserted, had put a violent end to her own existence'. The apparition then pointed to a clock which was just visible in the half-light, and announced that in three days to the minute Lord Lyttleton would be dead. Although shaken by the experience, the nobleman joked about it to his friends the following day and determined to 'bilk the ghost'. On the third night, his friends endeavoured to calm Lord Lyttleton by advancing the clocks in the house an hour, with the result that when the fatal moment apparently arrived he was much relieved to find himself unaffected. But on going to bed an hour later, just as a church clock nearby struck the real time, he sank into his valet's arms and died without a sound. A remarkable painting of the ghostly encounter, executed in 1780, is reproduced here; according to Sir Nathaniel Wraxall, an authority on the nobleman, it was 'faithfully designed after the description given to the artist by the *valet-de-chambre* who attended Lord Lyttleton and to whom his master related all the circumstances'.

It is towards the end of the eighteenth century that we begin to find the first authenticated American ghost stories. One early example, set in 1774 during the War of Independence, concerns a spirit that was 'Heard, But Not Seen', to quote the title of a contemporary account.

Two British officers were awaiting the return of a Major Blomberg who was out on a foraging party; eventually, their patience all but exhausted, they heard his familiar footsteps approaching outside the tent. However, instead of entering the Major seemed to pause outside. A voice then

Above: The famous painting of the ghost which appeared to Lord Lyttleton in November 1779 bringing news of his imminent death

addressed the men instructing one of them that when he returned to England he was to go to a certain house in Westminster; there, in a room which the voice minutely described, he would find papers of great importance to the Major's ten-year-old son. The footsteps then turned and faded away into the distance. Puzzled by their friend's behaviour, the two soldiers rushed out of the tent – but there was no sign of the Major. A guard on duty was questioned, but insisted he had neither seen nor heard anyone. As they stood talking, a party emerged from the woods carrying a man's corpse. It was that of Major Blomberg, who had been killed about ten minutes earlier. The body had been struck by three bullets causing instant death, and it could only be concluded that the Major had addressed his friends in one place at the very time of his death in another.

The bizarre story did not end there – for on his return to England, the friend searched the house in Westminster and found deeds to property in Yorkshire, which the Major had hidden away as an inheritance for his son. The event became the topic of much society gossip on both sides of the Atlantic; Queen Charlotte herself was so intrigued by it that she had the young Blomberg brought up in the Royal Nursery and employed Gainsborough to paint his portrait as a memorial to the phantom who was 'heard, but not seen'.

The second story from North America was described by Robert Owen, the eighteenth-century statesman and American Ambassador at the court of Naples, as 'as clear an instance of the truth of an apparition of the dead as it is possible for the mind to conceive'. The tale is set on the island of Cape Breton in October 1785. Two young soldiers, Sherbroke and Wynyard – later to become Sir John Sherbroke and General John Wynyard – were studying late one night in their quarters when the figure of a tall youth about twenty years old appeared before them. Severely emaciated, the figure was also lightly clothed, unlike the soldiers who wore heavy furs against the cold.

Sherbroke's gaze passed from the figure to his friend. 'I have often heard' he later wrote, 'of a man being as pale as death, but I never saw a living face assume the appearance of a corpse as Wynyard's did at that moment.' Both watched spellbound as the figure stared for some moments at Wynyard before passing through one of the doors. There was a moment's silence and then Wynyard spoke. 'Why, good God, that was my brother!' Both knew this to be impossible, for the brother was in England – but the most careful search of the quarters failed to throw any light on the mystery. Having made the most detailed notes of the occurrence, the men decided to write to England for news of Wynyard's brother. However, when the reply finally arrived it only served to deepen the mystery – for the younger Wynyard had apparently died in London at just the moment when he was seen staring at his brother in Canada! Throughout the rest of their lives, both Sherbroke and Wynyard were frequently asked about their strange experience; both retained the unshakable conviction that they had indeed seen a ghost of the dead.

A third and final American ghost which should be mentioned here is the poltergeist which attached itself to the family of Dr Thorn in New Haversak, New York, in 1789. In March of that year strange knocking sounds began to be heard and items were thrown about the house; these manifestations continued for some months and were ·investigated by several churchmen and theologians, but they were never explained. A white-clad figure was also said to have appeared to one of the serving girls, but as she was reputedly of a highly emotional and suggestive nature, her report was not taken seriously. It did serve however as the basis for several dramatic ghost prints, one of which is reproduced here.

In Europe too, there were a number of well-recorded ghostly visitations during the eighteenth century. In Germany in 1721 the renowned Oriental scholar Professor Schupart was for some months subjected to the attentions of a poltergeist in his home at Groben. The spirit hurled around household objects and stones, some weighing more than ten pounds, and so interfered with the Professor that he could not undress and sleep in his bed for over a month. His wife was also bitten, pinched and knocked down by the spirit. The unfortunate scholar invited several groups of people to his home to witness these extraordinary events, and on one occasion no fewer than twelve witnesses saw a violent attack on the Professor 'by invisible hands that did him much hurt'.

A similarly wicked spirit was also at work in France in the shop and home of M. Dupoirier at St Medard during 1734. A committee appointed by the Commissary to report on the incidents saw stones thrown both inside and outside the buildings but could provide no natural explanation. In 1746 a similar phenomenon occurred in Amiens which was witnessed by several local dignitaries, including Father Charles Richard. Many people are said to have heard noises and seen stones being thrown, and as the incidents continued for about fourteen years this easily qualifies as the longest continuous poltergeist haunting on record.

Interesting ghost stories are also to be found in Sweden and Russia: the weird figure of the Devil of Hjalta-Stad, who appeared in that small Swedish community in 1750, almost causing a mass exodus; and the Bell-Ringing Ghost of the Russian monastery of Tzarekonstantinoff, who in 1753 defied all attempts at exorcism and thoroughly disrupted life in the religious order for well over a year.

At the close of the eighteenth century men of science and learning began to make really concerted efforts to study the subject of apparitions. It was agreed that a good many spectral appearances could be put down to physical causes, or to simple cases of delusion and tricks of the light such as the Spectre of the Broken. Indeed, some of the first investigators, like Dr James Alderson, were anxious to prove that there was not the slightest grain of truth in any of the ghost stories. 'Such phenomena', he wrote in his journal in 1791, 'are not caused by the perturbed spirits of the departed but are due to the diseased organisms of the living.' He supported this view with tales of men who had allegedly seen ghosts and were proved to have been under the influence of drink, and old ladies troubled by spirits which only appeared when they suffered an attack of the gout.

Another enquirer, Professor Hufeland of Jean, conducted a number of

A delightfully romantic interpretation of a ghost which was said to have appeared to a serving girl at the home of Dr Thorn in New Haversack, New York, in 1789

56

Right: The bizarre ghost known at 'The Devil of Hjalta-Stad' which appeared in Sweden in 1750

experiments in self-induced mental delusion and quoted the case of a Berlin bookseller, Nicolai, who could will spirits to appear. Hufeland himself achieved the same sensations and reported in 1799, 'While in the full use of my senses, even in the greatest composure of mind, for almost two months constantly and involuntarily, I saw a number of human and other apparitions, nay I even heard voices; yet after all, this was nothing but the consequence of nervous debility or irritation or some unusual state of the system.' The Professor added that the apparitions were all of people he knew – either living or dead, but 'paler than in nature' – and that he had conversed with them 'as realizing they were phantoms'. 'Thus' wrote a third enquirer, John Abercrombie, the Scottish physician, 'intense mental conceptions strongly impressed upon the mind, are for the moment believed to have a real existence.'

Abercrombie and others noted how ghosts had a habit of appearing at times when the mind was least prepared for a careful assessment of such phenomena. 'They appear,' one of these men observed, 'at night or in the hours of darkness when the human mind is susceptible to phantastic impressions. The midnight hour is the favoured period, and they are rarely seen by more than one person at a time, for it is often loneliness and concentration of thought that gives rise to phantasmagoria.' But even such authority and scepticism could not destroy a tradition as long-standing as that of ghosts. And while further enquiry in the nineteenth century, and indeed right up to the present time, has brought much new knowledge to the subject, apparitions have continued to appear and mankind to puzzle – and sometimes believe.

# 6.
# GHOST SHOWS, PHANTOM SHIPS AND THE BIRTH OF SPIRITUALISM

'A *decemvir* of the Republic has said that the dead return no more, but go to Robertson's exhibition and you will soon be convinced of the contrary, for you will see the dead returning to life in crowds. Robertson calls forth phantoms and commands legions of spectres.' So wrote the French journalist and Representative Armand Poultier in 1798, describing one of the most extraordinary phenomena in the history of apparitions. The ability to create ghostly figures by artificial means can, of course, be traced back to Roman times, but it was not until the early nineteenth century that it became an art which baffled and amazed people throughout Europe. As another facet of our history of ghosts it well deserves comment.

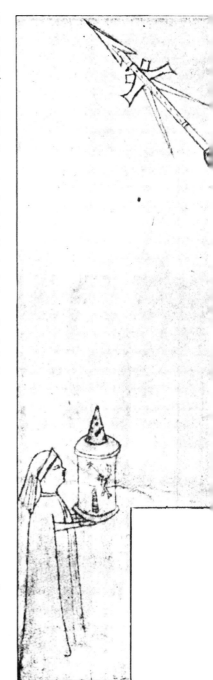

One master of this art of illusion was a Belgian optician, Etienne-Gaspard Robertson, who came to Paris in the aftermath of the French Revolution determined to profit personally from the chaos of society. In 1794 he addressed a government meeting in which he proposed the construction of a gigantic burning glass to set fire to the English fleet, at that time blockading the French seaports. Not surprisingly, this plan found little support, so instead he decided to capitalize on his inventiveness and knowledge of optical illusions by creating a 'ghost-making-machine' to amuse the local population and exploit their innate fear of the supernatural. His 'Phantasmagoria' was set up at the Pavilion de l'Echiquier where Robertson himself appeared before the audience dressed all in black, speaking dolefully of sorcery, magic and ghosts and offering to raise the dead. Armand Poultier was present at one such gathering and described it thus:

'I was seated in a well-lighted apartment with sixty or seventy people. At seven o'clock a pale, thin man entered the room and having extinguished the candles, he said, 'Citizens, I am not one of those adventurers and impudent swindlers who promise more than they can perform. I have assured the public in the *Journal de Paris* that I can bring the dead to life, and I shall do so. Those of the company who desire to see the apparitions of those who were dear to them, but who have passed away from this life by sickness or otherwise, have only to speak; and I shall obey their commands.' There was a moment's silence, and a haggard-looking man, with dishevelled hair and sorrowful eyes, rose in the midst of the assemblage and exclaimed, 'As I have been unable in an official journal to re-establish the worship of Marat, I should at least be glad to see his shadow.' Robertson immediately threw upon a brazier containing lighted coals, two glasses of of blood, a bottle of vitriol, a few drops of aquafortis, and two numbers of the *Journal des Hommes Libres*, and there instantly appeared in the midst of the smoke caused by the burning of these substances, a hideous livid phantom armed with a dagger and wearing a red cap of liberty. The man at whose wish the phantom had been evoked seemed to recognize Marat, and rushed forward to embrace the vision, but the ghost made a frightful grimace and disappeared. A young man next asked to see the phantom of a young lady whom he had tenderly loved, and whose portrait he showed to the worker of all these marvels. Robertson threw upon the brazier a few sparrow's feathers, a grain or two of phosphorus, and a dozen butterflies. A beautiful woman with her bosom uncovered and her hair floating about her, soon

Above: Probably the oldest recorded use of a magic lantern – the simple apparatus designed by Johannes de Fontana (c.1420) projected a picture which was drawn on blackened cylindrical glass

Previous page: Contemporary illustration for Johann von Schiller's novel about phantom illusions, *The Ghost-Seer*

appeared, and smiled on the young man with most tender regard and sorrow. A grave-looking individual sitting close to me suddenly exclaimed, 'Heavens! it's my wife come to life again,' and he rushed from the room, apparently fearing that what he saw was not a phantom.'

Robertson's marvels were soon the sensation of Paris and despite at least one attempt by the police to ban his exhibitions 'because they traffic unlawfully with the dead', he was soon searching for a larger venue to accommodate the huge crowds. An abandoned chapel full of tombs and funeral tablets at the Capuchin convent near the Place Vendome provided just the right setting. He draped the place in black and suspended from the ceiling a sepulchral lamp in which alcohol and salt were burned, giving forth a ghastly light which made the faces of the spectators resemble those of corpses. At the performances, here he would first address the audience and then plunge the chapel into complete darkness. A storm of wind, rain, thunder and lightning followed, interspersed with the tolling of a church bell; after this the solemn strains of a far-off organ were heard. Summoned by the conjuror, phantoms of Voltaire, Mirabeau, Jean-Jacques Rousseau, Robespierre, Danton, all appeared and faded away again 'into thin air'. The ghost of Robespierre was shown rising from a tomb. A flash of lightning, vivid and terrible, would strike the phantom, whereupon it would sink down to the ground and vanish. It was not unusual for people to rush screaming from the exhibitions, or for women to be carried out in a faint. Great credence was given to Robertson's 'ghosts' and it was to be some years before his secret use of concave mirrors and convex lens, concealed assistants and props was revealed. All this knowledge had of course been garnered during his earlier work in the science of optics, and the various illustrations on the pages here clearly show the workings of his equipment.

Such was his success that variations of Robertson's show were to appear throughout Europe, and miniature versions called Phantascopes which could duplicate the illusion were in time developed for home use. The great German poet Johann Friedrich von Schiller used the idea of ghost-making apparatus as the basis for his novel *The Ghost-Seer* which became one of the most popular of all Gothic novels. It is also mentioned in Charles Dickens's *Christmas Carol* and *The Haunted Man;* in Bulwer Lytton's *Strange Story* and Alexander Dumas's *Corsican Brothers*.

Perhaps the greatest of all these 'ghost shows' was evolved in London later in the century and first demonstrated by Professor John Henry Pepper in 1863. It was a great advance on the earlier exhibitions in that it projected moving figures into the air. The Professor had done away with mirrors and magic lanterns and simply used a large sheet of unsilvered glass. The trick was based on a well-known optical illusion whose principle Pepper explained in a later essay:

In the evening carry a lighted candle to the window and you will see reflected in the pane, not only the image of the candle, but that of your hand and face as well. A sheet of glass, inclined at a certain angle, is placed on a stage and just in front of the glass, is a person robed in a white shroud, and illuminated by the brilliant rays of the electric or the oxy-hydrogen light. The image of the actor who plays the part of the spectre, being reflected by the glass, becomes visible

61

to the spectators, and stands, apparently, just as far behind the glass as its prototype is placed in front of it. This image is only visible to the audience. The actor who is on the stage sees nothing of it, and in order that he may not strike at random in his attacks on the spectre, it is necessary to mark beforehand on the boards the particular spot at which, to the eyes of the audience, the phantom will appear. Care must be taken to have the theatre darkened and the stage very dimly lighted.

Despite efforts to patent these improvements, Professor Pepper's show was soon being extensively copied; perhaps the best of the imitators was the French conjuror, Robin, whose shows drew huge audiences in Brussels, Vienna, Rome, Munich and Venice. He terrified onlookers with spectres rising from graveyards to embrace the living, with devils taunting musicians unable to seize them, and oriental phantoms fencing with living mortals.

The accompanying illustrations and diagrams of the Pepper and Robin illusions serve well to demonstrate the principles employed by the veritable army of nineteenth-century ghost-makers. The 'creating' of ghosts emerged in yet another form later on in the same century when the magic lantern evolved into the camera. This, as we shall see, was to produce the remarkable and bizarre 'spirit photographs'.

Aside from these artificial manifestations, the real ghosts – if the reader will accept the existence of such beings – were still making their regular and baffling appearances. In the winter of 1804 a phantom created a sensation in London and spread fear throughout the capital. The Hammersmith Ghost so alarmed the people of that district that few would venture

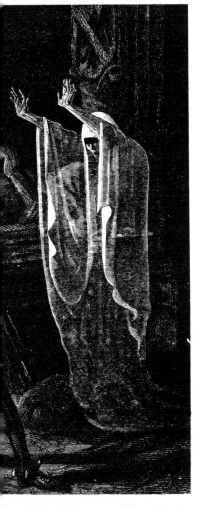

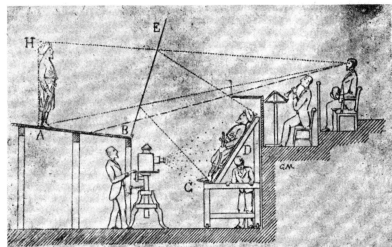

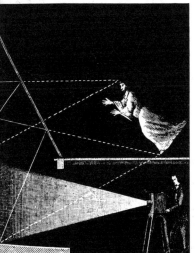

Far left: A small-scale version of Robertson's illusion which could create exciting effects for wide-eyed family audiences

Left: Professor John Henry Pepper's famous 'Ghost Illusion'. The first picture shows the illusion as it was seen by the audience, and the drawing reveals how Professor Pepper utilized a lamp and a sheet of unsilvered glass to create the effect. A similar technique to Professor Pepper's was employed by the French conjuror Robin as the two illustrations above reveal

THE HI...
*Mysteri...*
And alarm...
AT THE CORNER OF STAN...
Well known to have been u...
The Skele...
ALSO THE
FEMALE
Which app...
And an acco...
VICTIMS OF SEDU...
The wonder and excitement caus...
by ...
Extraordinary Disa...
Alarming noises and strange shadows ;...
account of what has bee...
*Skeleton an...*
THE REPORT OF THE BU...
And other interesting particulars. S...
FATE OF T...
Supposed to be a tenant many years a...
in the country, and the co...

LONDON : PUBLISHED BY W. JE...
And Sold...

Left: 'The Hammersmith Ghost' as it was pictured in the *Wonderful Magazine* of 1804

f THE

*House*

pearances

T., BLACKFRIARS ROAD,

many Years, and called

's Corner !

S OF THE

PECTRE

Window ;

who are the

N AND MURDER.

pearance of the house, and also

nd

ance of the Inmates.

exited on passing the house, and an

have been seen of the ?

pparitions.

KER, AND THE PIEMAN,

that strange Female in Black, and

UNG LADY

account of an old haunted Mansion

yed by a young Officer.

01, LEATHER LANE, HOLBORN,

sellers.

Above: Title page of the pamphlet about the bizarre events which occurred in a building in Blackfriars, London, in the 1820s

out after dark. According to reports, one of its first appearances was to a woman crossing the local churchyard late at night. She saw a very tall white figure rise from behind one of the tombstones, and when she ran away it pursued her, seizing her by the arms, whereupon she fainted. She was later found and taken home; but apparently she never got over the shock and died within a few days.

The ghost's next appearance was to a transport wagon carrying sixteen people, all of whom fled at the sight of it. Twice more the spectre terrified late-night passers-by, and so enquiries into the matter were instituted by the local authorities. A theory was advanced that the spectre was that of a young man who had cut his throat in the neighbourhood; but no one immediately volunteered to find out by personal confrontation.

However, such was the panic which thereafter spread through the Hammersmith district that a group of bolder residents decided to set up a vigilante committee to settle the mystery once and for all. For three nights the men lay in wait around the churchyard, but nothing happened; then, on the fourth night, one of the watchers, an excise officer named Francis Smith, saw a figure in white advancing towards him down Black Lion Lane. He stepped out of the bushes and fired at the advancing form with his shotgun. Men tumbled out of their hiding-places and clustered around the groaning body. But it was no ghost: Smith had shot an unfortunate bricklayer named Thomas Milwood returning late from work in his white overalls! Smith was later sent for trial on a charge of manslaughter, but after being found guilty and sentenced to death, was pardoned and given a year's imprisonment instead. 'The Ghost', a contemporary historian wrote, 'was never discovered and is still living.'

Pamphlets and broadsheets of this period indicate that interest in reports of ghosts ran high – two typical publications complete with engravings are reproduced here – but I doubt very much that there was a more extraordinary case committed to record than that of the various phantoms which inhabited the Mysterious House at Skeleton Corner about 1820.

The dwelling-place of this strange group of phantoms was the old and derelict corner building of Stamford Street in Blackfriars, London. This was a busy spot much frequented by prostitutes ('ladies who tarry on the corner', they were called), but the owner of the house, an eccentric old lady, had let it fall into disrepair. Hardly surprisingly it gained a reputation as being haunted; but it was not until the 1820s that strange, misty figures began to be seen at the broken windows. The first of these was a headless woman in white. No sooner had reports of this spectre begun to circulate, than another was spotted: this time a 'murderous-looking villain' with a razor in one hand and the head of a female apparently in a handkerchief in the other 'as if in the act of making an escape'. Other phantoms and skeletons subsequently appeared and stories were soon being told of bakers having loaves snatched from their barrows by invisible hands, and butcher's boys and piemen who had been relieved of their goods when they paused outside the house.

Some authorities insisted all the events were the work of vagrants who had taken up residence in the derelict building, but searches and constant watches failed to substantiate this theory. For years sightseers travelled from miles around to stand at Skeleton Corner and tales of the spectres proliferated. No satisfactory explanation of this mystery was ever advanced and records indicate that the figures continued to be seen until the building was finally demolished in 1878 to make way for a bank.

Controversy also surrounded the ghost which was first reported when the old Hampton Church at Hampton Court was demolished. There are several stories about ghosts at this royal palace, the luckless Jane Seymour and Kathryn Howard being only two of the restless spirits said to walk its corridors and lawns, but perhaps the best authenticated is that of Mistress Sibell Penn, nurse to Edward VI. Mistress Penn was taken ill with smallpox in 1562 (at the same time as Queen Elizabeth was suffering from the disease) and died on 6 November. She was buried in the old church and a monument was erected to her memory. Her bones then lay undisturbed for three centuries until the church was demolished in 1829 and her remains scattered. Shortly thereafter strange noises and mutterings were heard in the chamber of the palace where the old nurse had lived. Then the lady herself was seen, a tall and gaunt figure in a long grey robe with a hood over her head, her hands outstretched as if in appeal. Since that time the ghost of Mistress Penn has frequently terrified people in the palace, and in 1881 she particularly scared a sentry who said he saw her pass right through a wall! An anonymous artist who also witnessed the phantom at the close of the century has left us the sketch which is reproduced on these pages.

The other important British ghost story which should be mentioned here is that of the Bealing Bells which rang repeatedly for a period of fifty-four days in 1834 and have come to be regarded as one of the classic cases of poltergeist phenomena. The event took place at Great Bealings, a small village near Woodbridge in Suffolk, in the home of Major Edward Moor, a scholarly and unemotional man who was also a Fellow of the Royal Society. The bells hung in the kitchen of Major Moor's home and were used to summon the servants. Yet on the morning of 2 February the bells began to ring intermittently when no one was near, and continued to do so until 27 March, despite the most rigorous investigation and enquiry. Several groups of observers watched the rows of bells swinging back and forth and concluded that only ghostly hands could be moving them. To this day there has been no explanation as to why the bells were rung, or why they should have stopped as suddenly and mysteriously as they had begun.

In the early years of this century many writers and other practitioners of the arts became intensely interested in the old legends of phantom ships. Already by the early 1840s the most famous of these, the legend of the Flying Dutchman, had been drawn upon by Auguste Jal in his *Scenes de la Vie Maritime* (1832), Heinrich Heine in an essay of 1834 and Captain Marryat in *The Phantom Ship* (1839), as well as by Richard Wagner in his opera of the same name. Perhaps this opera, produced in 1834, did most to immortalize the legend: 'From that date' a commentator has written, 'the phantom sailor became a part of popular mythology, with the

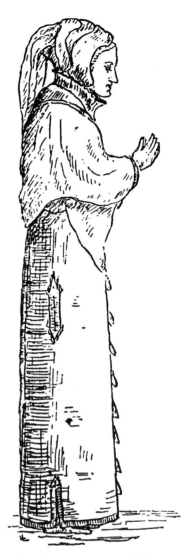

A 19th-century pen and ink sketch made by an anonymous artist of the ghost of Mistress Penn who walks the corridors of Hampton Court

curious result that seamen amongst whom the story probably originated, lost their fear of the ghostly vessel.'

The origins of the legend were founded in the story of a Dutch captain who, attempting to sail his ship around the Cape of Good Hope in a raging storm, defied everyone – both his crew and the Almighty – to sink him. For his blasphemy he was condemned to sail the seas for ever in his phantom ship, luring other vessels and their crews to their doom. In time, it was said, the captain repented, but his crew had by then been turned to skeletons and were deaf to all his pleas.

Many sailors have told of sighting this vessel, but perhaps the most famous witness was Prince George (later to become George V, the grandfather of the present Queen), who described seeing it on 11 July 1881 when sailing as a young naval cadet in H.M.S. *Inconstant*, in a fleet off the south coast of Australia. He recorded the incident in the ship's log which is now preserved by the Admiralty in London:

> At 4 a.m. 'The Flying Dutchman' crossed our bows. She emitted a strange phosophorescent light as of a phantom ship all aglow, in the midst of which light the masts, spars and sails of a brig 200 yards distant stood out in strong relief as she came up on the port bow where also the officer of the watch from the bridge saw her, as did also the quarter-deck midshipman, who was sent forward at once to the forecastle, but on arriving there no vestige nor any sign whatever of any material ship was to be seen either near or right away to the horizon, the night being clear and the sea calm.

According to the young Prince the number of men on board the *Inconstant* who saw the phantom ship was thirteen; and its sighting may well have been an omen of the inexplicable deaths of a young sailor and the Admiral of the Fleet which followed shortly thereafter.

Writers who have studied this legend and similar tales of the sea have learned that phantom ships were featured in the mythology of many countries including Britain, Germany, Scandinavia, America and even China. Their researches have produced many familiar and still popular yarns.

One of the most interesting modern stories of ghost ships tells of a vessel which haunts the North American coast. The *Palatine*, a Dutch immigrant ship, originally sailed for the New World in 1752, but ran into tremendous storms off Rhode Island which battered it unmercifully and resulted in the death of the captain. The crew then robbed the ship and took to the life-boats leaving the passengers to fend for themselves. For some days the *Palatine* drifted helplessly until it finally ran aground on Block Island. There the inhabitants allowed the immigrants to land, then plundered the vessel and set fire to it, leaving one demented passenger who refused to land still aboard. Blazing fiercely, the ship was set adrift and disappeared over the horizon. Every year thereafter on the anniversary of the looting a ghostly ship blazing from stem to stern has been said to glide along the coast past Block Island.

Authentic stories of ghosts on board ships are by no means as plentiful as those about phantom vessels. Sir Walter Scott does record one of a seaman who was shot and killed by the captain of a Liverpool slaver and

Phantom ships have been a recurring legend of the sea as these examples show. The old print (left) was made at the start of the 19th century and illustrates a tradition which was already generations old. The *Marie Celeste* (below) was found deserted, and it has been suggested that her crew and passengers were driven overboard by a poltergeist. The *Flying Dutchman* (top right) is perhaps the most famous of all phantom ships, and among those who have seen her was George V when he was a young naval cadet. The *Palatine* (bottom right) is America's best known contribution to this enduring tradition

# AN ACCOUNT

### OF THE

# DREADFUL APPARITION

That appeared last night to Henry —— in this street, of Mary ——, the shopkeeper's daughter round the corner, in a shroud, all covered in white.

The castle clock struck one—the
drear, and tempestuous. — He
chamber of it, over a woo
of contemplation, he h
lifeless embers;
Mary—the
disclos

### PARTICULARS

## Of a Singular and Curious Circumstance

Which took place at the House of a well known

# FORTUNE TELLER,

With the strange appearance that was witnessed,

Last night the following curious circumstance took place in a house in this neighbourhood, which occasioned a great deal of merriment. Six young women, whose names are as follows:—Jane Trustsoot, Ann Dingle, Mary Prause, Priscilla Richards, Harriett Pridhame, and Mary Twining, having previously agreed together, went to the residence of a notorious fortune teller about nine o'clock, to dive into the history of their future destiny, or if possible, to gain information respecting their intended husbands or future sweethearts. On entering his apartment, the said girls became rather abashed, but after hearts had passed between them, this cards of cards began his curious oracle, which con-
in unintelligible
k of cards
placed

consulted his oracle, he then related unto them their destiny. The enquiring girls wished to know if he could not tell the names of their sweethearts; he answered in the affirmative, and said, if they would give him 2s. 6d each, he would bring them into the room; the girls said they had not so much, and he told them to raise what they could, which amounted in all to 3s. 6d. They were the placed in a ring, and the ol man began muttering som words and shuffling his card , when three loud knocks were heard at the door. The sounds appeared to proceed from the stair-case. Shortly after the knocking had ceased, the door slowly opened, and the figure of a tall man with an unnatural cast of countenance entered the room and took a seat opposite the affrighted maids. The appearance had a white ghastly head, and was dressed in the style of a cavalier of the time of Charles II; but what was most remarkable, the body was a mere shadow, it was a thing of vapour, for the back of the chair was plainly discernible through it. It raised its hand three times in a menacing attitude, three times at the young women, which so alarmed them, that they all commenced screaming and wildly ran from the room—the house was aroused— the police was called in—but no trace of the apparition was visible, unless a curious odour which perfumed the apartment might be considered so.

Disley, Printer, 57, High Street, St. Giles.

27

Two of the many broadsheets about ghosts and other strange events which were sold on the streets of London and large towns and cities in the 19th century

The two American sisters
whose ghostly experience
was to give birth to
Spiritualism: Margaret Fox
(top) and her younger sister,
Kate

returned to haunt his murderer so effectively that he finally threw himself overboard and drowned. As the captain disappeared beneath the waves, says Sir Walter, he was heard to call to his mate 'By God, Bill! He is with me now!' Lord Byron also noted the story of the commander of a packet ship, the *Captain Kidd*, who was visited by a phantom which sat on his bed and was damp to the touch. The spirit was said to have been that of the commander's brother who had been drowned in the Indian Ocean.

It has been suggested that the famous mystery of the *Marie Celeste* (1872) could have been the work of a ghost, or more specifically, a poltergeist. The case of this American brigantine, found drifting and apparently hastily abandoned between Lisbon and the Azores, has been widely discussed; but it was the late Harry Price who first suggested in 1945 that a vicious spirit might have driven both the passengers and crew into the sea. He cited several other cases where ghosts were believed to have brought disaster to ships, including the pamphlet *A true and Perfect Account of a Strange and Dreadful apparition which lately Infested and Sunk a Ship bound for Newcastle* (1672), and added, 'It is just a possibility. If poltergeists can cause people to abandon their homes (as they have done frequently), they can surely make life equally unbearable aboard ship.'

The most important single event in the nineteenth century as far as our history of ghosts is concerned – indeed it is also one of the most significant events in supernatural history as a whole – concerns two American sisters and 'The Ghost Story which Started Spiritualism'. The setting for this amazing event – which 'kindled a fire from which the flame of a new reformation sprang and spread all over the world', to quote Dr Nandor Fodor – was a broken-down wooden house in the small rural community of Hydesville in Wayne County in New York State. There lived John D. Fox, a poor farmer, with his wife and two children, Margaret, ten, and Kate, seven, all of whom were devout Methodists.

On a March morning in 1848, strange raps and knocks were heard in the house; they continued throughout the following days and nights, gaining in intensity, until by the end of the month the whole building was literally being shaken to its rickety foundations. Quite by chance, while the knocking was going on, little Kate clapped her hands; almost immediately there was an answering clap. She snapped her fingers: back came a snapping sound. Margaret then clapped – and was similarly answered. She ran in amazement to fetch her parents.

John Fox and his wife were perhaps not as surprised at their young daughter's story as most parents might have been for they had already learned that their home had the reputation of being haunted, and deduced that the sound must be being made by some unhappy and restless spirit. They therefore followed the lead of Kate and Margaret and attempted to communicate with the ghost by means of a series of knocks. As a result of that simple act the family changed the traditional attitude towards ghosts; for in return the spirit attempted to convey an intelligent message to them, something which had never previously been recorded.

First, the spirit rapped out the ages of the Fox children, and then, knocking twice as the letters of the alphabet were read out, told its own gruesome story. It emerged the ghost was that of a pedlar named Charles Rosma, who had stayed one night in the house and been murdered by his host. His body had then been buried in the cellar and all signs of his visit obliterated. Here, the rapping said, he was doomed to stay until someone found his remains.

News of this amazing communication was quickly given to the authorities by John Fox, and a search was ordered. Sure enough, in the cellar were the remains of a human body. Within days the Fox's wooden home attracted hundreds of visitors seeking to hear the ghost which could communicate from 'The Other Side'.

Even with all this excitement, the story had really only just begun. On subsequent nights the sounds of a death-struggle and of a heavy body being dragged across the floor were added to the knockings. The Fox family began to fear for their sanity. They decided to abandon the house and went to stay with friends, while sightseers by the hundred moved into the vicinity and continued to 'talk' with the spirit.

When, finally, someone thought to ask the ghost if it had a message to impart, the response was immediate. 'Dear friends,' the reply came in knocks, 'you must proclaim the truth to the world. This is the dawning of a new era; you must not try to conceal it any longer. When you do your duty, God will protect you and good spirits will watch over you.'

Many Americans – indeed a great many people throughout the world – were anxiously awaiting some message about the hereafter, for the new Darwinian theory of evolution was already undermining the traditional religious view that man had an immortal spirit. Therefore the discovery of the Fox sisters that the dead not only still existed in spirit form but could actually communicate with the living was welcomed with great joy and an almost total lack of scepticism. Disciples in their thousands quickly flocked to Spiritualism, as the religion was soon called, and Margaret and Kate Fox became national celebrities. In a few years, conversing with spirits – by rapping, automatic writing, speaking while under hypnosis, and, finally, by manifestation when the ghost appeared in visible form – became a craze throughout America and Europe.

The Fox sisters spent the rest of their lives at the centre of controversy, alternately hailed as messiahs and condemned as frauds. Being constantly in the public gaze was to have an unsettling effect on both of them, and in 1888, amid a welter of publicity, they actually confessed to having invented the entire story of the communicating ghost. Many felt that this would be the end of the short-lived cult of Spiritualism; but almost immediately there came a further startling admission from Margaret. She announced that the sisters, who were in financial difficulties, had been promised a large sum of money to declare themselves frauds; but since the amount had proved less than expected, both now retracted their confessions.

That the two women ended their lives in squabbling and abortive attempts to raise money, undoubtedly cast a shadow over the new religion. But Spiritualism did nevertheless survive, and it was not long before it gave rise to some of the most remarkable pieces of evidence in man's perennial quest to meet the shades of the departed: the strange and highly controversial 'spirit photographs'.

Above: Kate Fox demonstrates to her parents how she and her sister communicate with the ghost in their house at Hydesville (from a drawing by S. Drigin)

Right: The Fox sisters
demonstrate their ability to
communicate with spirits
by levitating a table at a
seance in Rochester, New
York in 1850. Below: A
sardonic comment on
Spiritualism from a French
work *Mystères de la Séance*
in which the wrong spirit
has been materialized!

# 7.
# SPIRIT
# PHOTOGRAPHS
# - REAL OR FAKE?

The basic tenets of the new religion of Spiritualism were that people lived on after death and that their spirits could make contact with the world of the living through mediums. Spiritualists implicitly believed in the actuality of ghosts, and many could claim to have seen or heard relatives who had 'passed over' at the gatherings or seances which were held for just such communication.

The mediums were people gifted with the ability to make contact with the dead, in either physical or mental form: 'physical' mediums could cause the spirits to move or levitate objects, tap out communications and even on occasion materialize, while 'mental' mediums allowed the dead to take possession of their bodies and speak through them or guide their hands to write messages. (It is not unknown to find a medium capable of both these activities, just as there are Spiritualists who claim to sense the presence of a spirit without being able to communicate with it.) The seances at which contact with the dead was attempted normally involved two or more people, one invariably being the medium, who sat in a darkened room and linked hands to concentrate the 'psychic energy' required for a successful operation.

The aims and alleged achievements of Spiritualism have, of course, been the subject of endless conjecture since the days of the Fox Sisters, and it is not the purpose of this book to add further to the controversy. We should however examine the photographs which were allegedly taken of spirits materialized especially for the camera's eye.

Although the concept of photography dates back to Leonardo da Vinci, it was not until 1822 that Joseph Nicephore Niepce took what is now generally considered as the first photograph. The later work of Niepce, his son Isidore and Louis Daguerre (who on his own developed the daguerreotype) resulted in the plate camera which made the taking of pictures a skill available to everyone. For Spiritualists the camera obviously offered one way of proving to a sceptical public the truth of their claims. However, it is a matter of everlasting regret that so many charlatans battened on to the idea and that very little credence is now given to even the most carefully authenticated 'spirit photograph'. If we look at the case-histories of some of the famous 'spirit photographers' it is not difficult to see why.

The first person to produce such pictures was William H. Mumler, an American engraver and amateur photographer from Boston. He began experimenting in this area as early as 1860 and in 1862 released what he claimed was 'the first true photograph of a soul that has passed over'. Reproduced here for the first time in many years, it shows Mumler himself with the hazy but quite unmistakable form of a woman leaning comfortably against him. 'This photograph,' Mumler wrote in an accompanying statement, 'was taken by myself, on a Sunday, when there was not a living soul in the room beside me, so to speak. The form on my right I recognize as my cousin who passed away about twelve years since.'

The photograph, not surprisingly, caused a sensation: many Americans were eagerly receptive to the idea of psychical intervention and the art of the camera was still so new as to seem almost magical in itself. Immediately

Previous page:
One of the many hundreds of 'spirit photographs' which were produced in the latter half of the 19th century

76

Left: The first known
'spirit photographs' taken by
William Mumler of Boston,
showing himself and the
ghost of his cousin

Mumler was besieged with requests from all over America to duplicate
his 'art'. For some months he portrayed a variety of sitters with their
'extras' (as the ghostly figures came to be known), until, becoming over-
confident, he finally tripped himself up. He produced a spirit photograph
for a client in which the extra was recognized as a living person whom
Mumler had photographed only a few days before. As a result he was
prosecuted in New York in 1868 and the simple secret of his pictures was
revealed: he had superimposed the image of a second person on the
negative, and printed it in such a way that the 'ghost' came out in a hazy
shape. This revelation was a shattering blow to the Spiritualists who had
so eagerly championed Mumler's work; but it inspired a great many other
unscrupulous photographers in both America and Europe.

A Frenchman proved to be Mumler's most adept disciple, and he too
became much sought after in Europe in the late 1860s and 70s. This was
Edouard Buguet, whose pictures were masterpieces of clarity and clever
forgery. He began by using live models; but fearing that they might
expose him, he later switched to a dummy which he could dress up to
suit clients' expectations. Buguet also used cardboard dolls, beautifully

Mumler's techniques were
considerably improved upon
by the Frenchman
Edouard Buguet as the
photographs (below and
right) show – but, like
Mumler, he was exposed as
a fraud

The market for 'spirit photographs' spread far and wide. In Britain Richard Boursnell enjoyed considerable success until it was shown how he imposed photographs of the dead on to pictures of the living as this example (top) of a young soldier and his relatives proves. Heads and faces cut from newspapers and magazines (above) were the basic materials utilized by Mrs Ada Deane – until a group of footballers proved her downfall! Unlike these two, the beautiful South American medium, Madame Olivia (right), merely introduced 'psychic lights' into her photographs (top right) and enjoyed a long and successful career

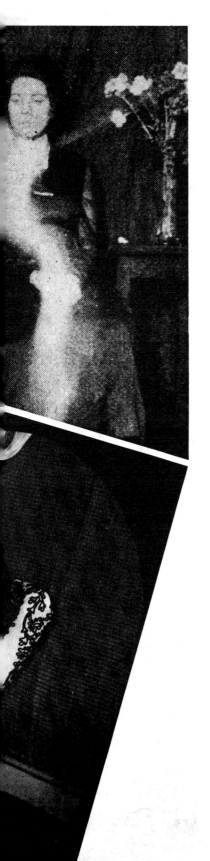

sculptured heads and garments of all kinds; and when in 1876 his studio was raided following complaints to the police by one disgruntled sitter his equipment spoke more eloquently than any confession of his deceit. He did confess, however, and among those who testified against him at his trial was the writer Flammarion. Buguet was found guilty and gaoled for a year. In spite of this exposure, his work was still held in high esteem in several quarters – his photographs, like the two reproduced here, rapidly became collector's items, and there were even those among his former customers who refused to believe that their pictures were faked.

Britain's most notorious practitioner of photographic deception was Richard Boursnell, who employed the same method of double exposure as Mumler in America, but would introduce an actual photograph of the deceased person if he could persuade the sitter to supply him with one. A typical example of his work, with the image of a dead soldier super-imposed on a picture of his wife and mother, is reproduced on these pages in the two stages of its 'production'.

It was not only men who concocted these photographs; a number of female mediums offered their services with the camera, notably Madam Olivia, the South American physical medium, and Mrs Ada Emma Deane, whose famous picture of faces floating around the Cenotaph on Armistice Day caused a sensation until she was exposed by the *Daily Sketch*. Madam Olivia, a beautiful and seductive Argentinian medium, did not take photographs of ghost figures, but 'psychic lights' through which, she said, it was possible to foretell the sitter's future. Although her famous portraits covered in strange white flashes were subsequently proved to have been doctored during the developing stages, her career as a medium was not seriously affected. Mrs Deane was a rather different personality: a former London charwoman, she had acquired an interest in photography from her brother and began by taking pictures of what she called 'Spirit Controls'. These beings were the ghosts of famous men and women of the past – often Red Indian chiefs or Egyptian princes – who could be summoned by anyone 'sensitive' enough to 'let them in' from the other side. By most standards her forgeries were crude, as the reproduced picture with its head cut from the front page of a magazine clearly shows; but she did for a time attract much public interest with her picture showing the heads of departed soldiers swirling around the Cenotaph in London on Armistice Day. However, the *Daily Sketch* rudely pricked the bubble by pointing out that the heads were in fact those of a number of living football players!

Newspapers were not alone in questioning the authenticity of spirit photographs, and on both sides of the Atlantic a number of investigators published authoritative studies of the phenomena. None, however, was quite as important as the great physicist Sir William Crookes (1832–1919), president of the Society for Psychical Research – the leading body for the investigation of all abnormal or supernatural occurrences – and a life-long enquirer into the mysterious. As Harry Price has written of him, 'It can be stated that it was Crookes who first demonstrated the need for a scientific technique when dealing with the physical phenomena of the seance-room and he was doing so as long ago as 1871.' Crookes's life has already been exhaustively detailed and his autobiography *Researches in the Phenomena of Spiritualism* (1874) is recommended reading to anyone pursuing a more complete study of the subject. His interest in Spiritualism seems to have begun with the Fox sisters in America, and he met Kate Fox and published an essay on the experiences of the two girls. But it was in connection with another girl that he was to earn his most enduring fame: Katie King, the 'spirit control' of a medium named Florrie Cook.

Florrie Cook was one of a great many mediums in London in the latter half of the nineteenth century, but she distinguished herself by claiming to raise the ghost of Katie King, the daughter of a pirate chief, John King. Crookes paid a number of visits to Florrie Cook's home where he witnessed the materialization of Katie King, and not only saw the spirit, but touched and embraced her. He carried out numerous scientific tests on Miss Cook, in one of which he placed her in an electric circuit broken by a galvanometer. The slightest movement of the medium, it was claimed, would have been recorded. But Katie appeared as usual, without the slightest deflection of the galvanometer needle being registered.

What Sir William considered the final proof of the authenticity of the spirit was a series of forty photographs he took of her, including one in which he himself appears with the girl clinging to his arm. Others showed her with members of Florrie Cook's circle looking on in some awe. (Most of the photographs were destroyed by Sir William's family at his death, but of those which survived the two best are reproduced here.) Critics were quick to compare the strikingly similar features of Florrie Cook and Katie, but Sir William remained a believer all his life, despite nearly losing his Fellowship of the Royal Society in the sensation caused by the publication of his report in 1874. It was even suggested at the time that Katie was in fact his mistress.

But while mediums like Florrie Cook only tried to convince small groups of their psychic abilities, two young Americans turned what they considered their 'mysterious powers' over spirits into a stage act which baffled and delighted audiences around the world. Ira and William Davenport, the sons of a New York State policeman, were contemporaries of the Fox sisters, and living near the girls' home, were among the first to hear of the ghostly communications in Hydesville. They, too, claimed to have heard strange noises in their home, but went further than the sisters in saying that they could actually make the spirits do their bidding. Experiments were thereafter carried out in which the brothers allowed themselves to be bound hand and foot, and still the noises persisted. Aware of the commercial value of their ability – whether they had a genuine mediumistic talent or were unashamed charlatans has never been satisfactorily proved – the Davenports developed a stage act which they took on a tour of the world. A picture of one of their performances which is reproduced here gives a clear indication of their act and underlines the claim that they were 'two of the most spectacular mediums of the nineteenth century'. (Another alleged medium who worked the halls of America and Europe in the wake of the Davenports was Josseffy, who climaxed his act by materializing a

The most famous 'spirit' to materialize for the camera was that of a pirate's daughter, Katie King. Among those who believed implicitly in her reality was the distinguished physicist Sir William Crookes, who was photographed with her several times. One of the few controversial pictures which was not destroyed is reproduced here (top). Another photograph of Katie taken by Sir William Crookes himself at a seance (above) shows Katie with another of her 'admirers', Dr Gulley of Malvern

Two pictures which began to strain public belief in spirit photography. Above: A photograph by the American medium, Captain Fawcett and (right) one of a series taken by an English photographer who specialized in graveyard portraits of the recently departed!

Left: The American brothers, Ira and William Davenport, who developed a stage act to demonstrate their powers over spirits. Right: A poster for advertising one of Ira Davenport's shows

ghostly figure he named 'The Spirit of Flowers'. See photograph.)

In the early years of the twentieth century, two names dominated the controversy over Spiritualism, and spirit photography in particular – the English writer and creator of the immortal Sherlock Holmes, Sir Arthur Conan Doyle, and the famed American 'Escapologist', Harry Houdini. Both developed a strong interest in the subject which lasted for many years, and Conan Doyle became as passionate a convert as Houdini was confirmed sceptic. Conan Doyle, who began his career as an obscure and penniless Southsea doctor, first became interested in psychical research as a young man and conducted some experiments in telepathy in 1887. He followed this up by attending a number of seances and in 1902 met Sir Oliver Lodge, the leading psychic investigator of the time; this proved one of the factors which caused him to abandon almost all his other activities and devote himself to Spiritualism immediately after the First World War. It has been suggested that the deaths of his wife (as a result of tuberculosis) and his younger son, Kingsley (through war wounds) made him unduly susceptible to the claims of the mediums with whom he came into contact, and that much of his writing on the subject resulted from fraud and deception perpetrated on him by others. Be that as it may, Conan Doyle was convinced when he heard the voice of his son at a seance conducted by a Welsh medium not long after the war, and then actually met and embraced the materialized spirit of his mother with the help of two American mediums, William and Eva Thompson. A few days later, though, these mediums were exposed at another seance

Left: Experts attempt to test the alleged powers of a medium in a cabinet of the same style as that used by the Davenport brothers

Right: The climax to the stage act of the American illusionist, Josseffy, who materialized a ghostly figure known as the 'Spirit of the Flowers'

by police officers, who found masks, wigs, chiffon, a musical box and
scent spray carefully hidden from view. The pastor of a Spiritualist
church, Leonard J. Hartman, made a detailed report of the scandal which
made fascinating reading.

Sir Arthur was not one to be easily shaken in his view, however, and
firmly convinced of life after death and the possibility of making contact with
spirits, he began to tour and lecture, showing not only spirit photographs
he had collected (including one of a 600-year-old inn at Norwich in which a
ghostly female form was visible) but others which he had taken or developed himself. He became particularly involved with a circle of spirit
photographers led by William Hope of Crewe. Of this man, and his fol-
lowers – who became known as the Crewe Circle – Doyle wrote in his
*The Case for Spirit Photography* (1922):

> Mr William Hope, who is a working man, discovered some seven-
> teen years ago, quite by chance, the remarkable power of producing
> extra faces, figures or objects upon photographic plates which had
> been given to him. In the first instance he was taking a fellow-
> workman, and the plate, when developed, was found to contain an
> extra figure which was recognised as being a likeness of his com-
> rade's sister, who had recently passed away. Since then many
> special tests have been demanded of him and have been successfully
> met. . . .
>
> That he has been fiercely attacked goes without saying, but each
> fresh allegation against him has ended in smoke, while his gifts have
> grown stronger with time. No medium can ever honestly guarantee
> success, but it would probably be within the mark if one claimed
> that Hope attained it three times out of five, though the results vary
> much in visibility and value.

The famous creator of
Sherlock Holmes, Sir Arthur
Conan Doyle, was a resolute
champion of spirit
photographs and appeared in
several such pictures himself.
Above: He appears in the
photograph of a female
enthusiast of his work.
Below: Posing with the
Crewe Circle for a
photograph taken by William
Hope in which a face has
materialized sideways! (The
head can be seen by turning
the book on its edge)

After his death, Sir Arthur Conan Doyle appeared in innumerable pictures by spirit photographers who believed his presence would convince the sitters of their authenticity

Conan Doyle found Hope a man of 'honesty and frankness' and posed for a number of pictures in which spirits appeared – all of which he believed to be genuine. The leading members of the Crewe Circle also posed for a group picture in which a face emerged sideways! (See photograph.)

Although he was submitted to 'inconvenience, losses and even insults' and forced to give up much of his paid work, Conan Doyle could not be discouraged from his belief. He joined several organizations including the British College of Psychic Science, and the Society for Psychical Research, and was vice-president of the delightfully-named Society for the Study of Supernormal Powers, whose members sold postcards of some of their best photographs to the general public. He also personally witnessed a ghost, received messages through the mediumship of his second wife about facts she could not possibly have known, and investigated a haunted house in Dorset. Of this adventure he later wrote, 'In the middle of the night a fearsome uproar broke out which made no impression upon the threads we had stretched across the doors and windows.' When the house later burned down, the skeleton of a child was found buried in the garden and Sir Arthur believed that her spirit had been responsible for the haunting, which after the fire was experienced no more.

In retrospect it seems clear that the famous writer was fooled by a great

These three pictures demonstrate more dramatically than words how spirit photographs could be created. They were produced by a British newspaper to show how it believed Sir Arthur had been fooled by the alleged pictures of the Cottingley Fairies. From the advertisement for Price's Night Lights (below) the fairy circle is cut out and then photographed on a blank plate (centre). This was then superimposed on the photograph of the great author to create quite a convincing effect (left)

Above: Another highly
successful American 'spirit
photographer' was William
Mullett of Los Angeles who
specialized particularly in
multiple images on his
pictures

Right: Harry Houdini, the
famous escapologist, was
deeply interested in
Spiritualism, but was
completely sceptical about
'spirit photographs'. This
picture, taken of him by
Alexander Martin of Denver
he called 'simply a double
exposure' (note the faces of
Lincoln and Roosevelt). In
his quest for the truth about
making contact with those
who had 'passed over',
Houdini attended many
seances all of which – like
the one here (right) where
he is partly hidden by an
alleged materialization –
failed to convince him

many Spiritualists and others interested in psychic phenomena. For instance, it is extremely difficult to understand his whole-hearted endorsement of the photographs allegedly showing fairies taken by two young girls in the village of Cottingley in Yorkshire; but against this one must balance the powers of deduction and reasoning which he displayed to such effect in the Sherlock Holmes stories. It is easy to dismiss his enquiries into Spiritualism because of the extreme nature of some of his cases; more difficult to disprove that he was at least partially right in some of his theories about 'the other side'.

Like Sir Arthur Conan Doyle, Harry Houdini was interested in occult phenomena for much of his life, and entered into Spiritualism in the hope of making contact with his beloved mother. The amazing career of Houdini, who was born Eric Weiss, involved some of the greatest escapes from seemingly impossible situations that the world has ever seen. Mystery being very much part of his stock-in-trade, it is not surprising to learn that he deliberately sought out mediums in the hope of penetrating their particular secrets. Over a period of thirty years he read everything he could find on the subject, attended innumerable seances in America, Britain and Europe, and discussed the matter with mediums and sceptics alike. Then, in his *A Magician Among The Spirits* (1924) he announced, 'In all that time I have not found one incident that savoured of the genuine. If there had been any really unalloyed demonstration to work on, one that did not reek of fraud, one that could not be reproduced by earthly powers, then there would be something for a foundation, but up to the present time everything that I have investigated has been the result of deluded brains or those which were too actively and intensely willing to believe.'

Houdini set out on his enquiry desperately wanting, as he admitted, to believe, in the hope of making contact with his dead mother's spirit. He was particularly impressed with the work of Sir Arthur Conan Doyle and Sir Oliver Lodge, and at various times in his life made solemn arrangements with older friends that they should try to contact him from the hereafter when they died. 'But I never received a word' he wrote. Conan Doyle tried to convince him that he was failing to achieve any results because his scepticism precluded the right kind of mental approach, but even a determined series of sessions with spirit photographers which produced some remarkable pictures failed to change his opinion one jot.

The best documented of these sessions was one Houdini had in 1923 with a Mr Alexander Martin of Denver, Colorado, who Conan Doyle had told him was 'a noted psychic photographer and a very wonderful man in this particular line'. The great escaper took along with him an assistant, and after talking to Martin for some time was invited into the photographer's studio.

> It was a simple room with a black background, and Martin pulled down a dark screen explaining that he did not need much light for the 'psychic stuff'. Then putting a shade on his eyes he turned to me, told me to sit and said, 'Now keep quiet and I will try and do something.' When he uncovered the lens I counted the time of exposure which was about fifteen seconds.

One of the cases which most fascinated Harry Houdini was that of the Boston medium 'Margery' (Mrs Le Roy Goddard Crandon), who claimed to materialize objects and receive messages from the dead. Top right: 'Margery' materializes a hand at a seance and (bottom right) some examples of the different styles of hand-writing and languages in which messages were transmitted through her while she was in a trance. Below: Cover of the book in which Houdini tried, without total success, to explain all 'Margery's' powers

After he covered it again he said to me, 'That is all I can do today. Now I must hurry away'. I thanked him and as I left I asked him if he had any photographs I could see. He gave me four to take away and study.

Houdini returned the following day to see what Martin had produced and was handed the photograph of himself with the semi-circle of misty faces which is reproduced here. He took the print back to his hotel, examined it carefully, then wrote: 'I have not the slightest doubt that Mr Martin's spirit photographs are simply double exposures. I think his method is to cut out various pictures, place them on a background and make an exposure. His plates are then ready for the next sitter, which in this case was me.' At this time, he added, there were rewards offered ranging from $500 to $5,000 for a spirit photograph that could be proved genuine – but not a single Spiritualist had come forward to try and claim the reward. 'From a logical, rational point of view,' he concluded in *A Magician Among the Spirits*, 'spirit photography is a more barefaced imposition and stands as evidence of the credulity of those who are in sympathy with the superstitions of occultism. It is also evidence of how unscrupulous mediums become and how calloused their consciences.'

Just as Conan Doyle had become associated with the leading psychical research bodies in England, so Houdini took members of the American Society for Psychical Research to task for their views and investigated many of their cases and mediums. The most famous of these cases concerned 'Margery', Mrs Le Roy Goddard Crandon of Boston, who claimed to be guided by the spirit of her brother, Walter, the victim of a railway accident. She could cause strange noises, produce trance-writing in nine languages, move objects about the room, materialize faces and take spirit photographs. Her exploits so caught the public's imagination that the *Scientific American* offered a prize of $2,500 for proof of her claims – or their exposure. A number of seances were held before a specially selected committee of observers, including Houdini, but no one was very impressed by what they witnessed. The enquiry eventually ended inconclusively when 'Margery' accused Houdini of deliberately trying to ruin her and refused to sit for the group again. Houdini thereafter published a report in which he detailed the tricks he said she employed to create her effects – and unsuccessfully claimed the *Scientific American*'s prize. The story did not end there, however, for 'Margery' also held seances in Europe and was visited by many of the leading researchers of the time. Views about her varied enormously, but no one ever completely demolished all her claims, and the woman's mediumship has with justification been called 'the most remarkable ever recorded'.

We should not close this section without some mention of another man who devoted much time and effort to spirit photographs and demonstrated just how they could be faked. He was the Englishman William Marriott, a professional magician and illusionist, who investigated many famous occult photographs and was also responsible for the exposure of a highly confidential organization supplying apparatus to fake mediums for their 'psychic tricks'. Although it was hotly denied that any such organi-

William Marriott, the scourge of the phony mediums, with some of the equipment they used to produce spirit materializations. Above: Fake hands with the handles which were invisible in the dark and (right) a complete set of equipment for a successful materialization

zation existed, Marriott managed to obtain one of its special catalogues from which mediums could select the equipment they needed. I am able to reproduce parts of it by courtesy of the Harry Price Library in London to whom it was donated. The booklet is entitled *Gambols With The Ghosts: Mind Reading, Spiritualistic Effects, Mental and Psychical Phenomena and Horoscopy* and was published in 1901 by the suppliers, Ralph E. Sylvestre of Chicago, who allowed it out only in private circulation and with the strict understanding that it was returned with all orders.

The 'miracles' which were for sale were described, but not explained, in the brochure. Success was guaranteed as 'our effects are being used by nearly all prominent mediums of the entire world', to quote Mr Sylvestre's introduction. 'For obvious reasons', the proprietor continued, 'we cannot mention the names of our clients and their work – they being kept in strict confidence, the same as a physician treats his patients.' Among the items on offer were slate-writing equipment, telescopic reaching-rods, self-playing guitars, trick ropes, fake padlocks, handcuffs, benches, self-rapping tables, and, for the beginner, a 'Complete Spiritualistic Seance'. Most ambitious of all, however, was the equipment for a ghostly materialization! The brochure listed it thus, 'For all materializing mediums, the production

"CABINET"

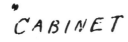

"CABINET"

Spirits usually materialized from the corner of rooms where seances were held. These two pictures by William Marriott reveal the whole trick. The hidden man or woman operated the 'spirit' from behind the curtains and, under cover of darkness, could cause the materialization to rise and then fall into nothingness as required

Another example of Marriott's exposures. Top right: A photograph of a young girl allegedly containing a message from the famous medium D. D. Home and (bottom right) the glass plate which was superimposed to create this effect

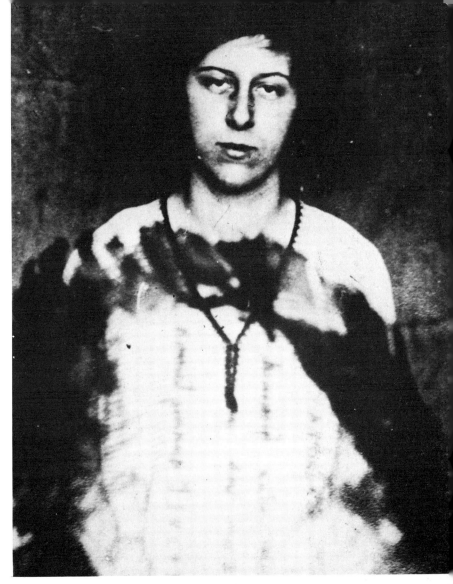

Spirit painting was yet another facet of the medium's 'art'. Marriott explained this painting (left) which, when the original was exposed to the light in a darkened room, showed a hidden figure emerging from the man's robes. The picture was the handiwork of the Bangs sisters of Chicago. Above: A faked 'spirit photograph' made by Marriott himself and (right) the firm believer, Sir Arthur Conan Doyle, forced into print at the end of his life to admit that spirit photography was not all that was claimed . . .

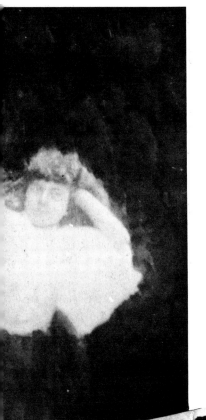

of luminous hands or faces is a *sina qua non* for their success. We furnish you complete with explicit directions for the making and production of same, or furnish them complete and ready for use as desired. Also draperies, head-dresses, and ornaments of the finest quality known. $5.00 to $25.00.' If the medium wanted to materialize a full-form apparition the cost was naturally higher: 'Luminous Materialistic Ghosts and Forms. All kinds and sizes. Full luminous female form and dress (with face that convinces) which can be produced in ordinary room or circle, appears gradually, floats about room and disappears. $50.00.' Marriott obtained and posed with several of these items, obviously causing acute embarrassment and annoyance to mediums who had invested their hard-earned money in them. He also produced his own spirit photographs, one particular example showing a delightful young girl apparently suspended on the crook of his arm!

The exposures by men like Marriott soon put an end to the work of most spirit photographers. But not to the photography of ghosts: indeed, as we shall see in our final chapter, the twentieth century has yielded a rich crop of examples from around the world.

## Mr. MARRIOTT'S DEMONSTRATION
### By SIR ARTHUR CONAN DOYLE.

Mr. Marriott has clearly proved one point, which is that a trained conjurer can, under the close inspection of three pairs of critical eyes, put a false image upon a plate. We must unreservedly admit it.

*Arthur Conan Doyle..*

# 8.
# GHOSTLY
# PHENOMENA TODAY

A census carried out by the Society for Psychical Research at the turn of the twentieth century indicated that approximately one person in sixteen saw or heard a ghost during his lifetime. This extraordinarily high figure was arrived at by the modern method of taking a cross-section of the public: some 17,000 people were canvassed, of whom 1,684 said they had had some form of supernatural experience. As with all such calculations, this result (nearly 10%) should be treated with caution; yet, just as the latest political opinion-poll can give us an indication of public attitudes, so can the 'ghost poll' highlight modern man's receptiveness to supernatural phenomena. Not everyone may believe in ghosts, but that a large proportion of the population is prepared to treat the subject seriously is clearly evident.

At the beginning of the new century, too, enquiry into all aspects of the occult was progressing more earnestly than ever, and throughout the western world new research organizations and societies burgeoned. Individuals also were exploring the various realms of the supernatural, and these years saw the publication of some of the most scholarly – often the definitive – works on topics like witchcraft, mysticism and ghosts. For the first time in centuries writers had gone back to original source material, rather than rewriting earlier books, and consequently much new speculation and alteration of opinion occurred. This trend has continued unabated to the present time when we are now questioning our very origins and even discussing the possibility that many of our ancient legends may reflect the visits to this planet of extra-terrestrial beings.

Despite continuing adverse publicity and the virtual shattering of all belief in spirit photographs, Spiritualism still flourished and when the movement celebrated its 100th anniversary it could boast 50,000 members in Britain and five times that number in America. Seances were being held more widely than ever and in an effort to convince the world of their genuineness several mediums allowed the materializations they produced in trances at these gatherings to be photographed. These materializations ranged from barely visible faces like wisps of smoke to fully formed and clothed bodies. They were said to grow out of a whitish substance known as ectoplasm (or teleplasm) that issued from one of the medium's orifices. It has to be noted that this substance bears a close resemblance to muslin or paste jelly, and these materials were certainly used as substitutes by fraudulent mediums, one of whom admitted that he had drawn his faces on gauze rolled in goose-fat.

The 1920s proved to be a heyday of enquiry into the reality of psychic phenomena. In retrospect it is amazing how the enemies of the movement directed the brunt of their attacks against the character of the medium or the enquirer, rather than what he or she was said to have achieved. Even investigators of the highest integrity found the merest inadequacy in their reports seized upon and used as an excuse for dismissing the entire matter. As one commentator has remarked bitterly, 'In no other field of study has the unequivocal testimony of so many witnesses of the highest calibre been discounted and written off as crass stupidity, or worse.' The reader interested in pursuing in depth this aspect of our history is directed

Previous page: 'The Spectre Monk', a photograph by the ghost-hunter and *Picture Post* photographer, Robert Thurston Hopkins

With the advances made in photography, ghost photographs became more convincing as these two specially created examples from the 1860s demonstrate

Several Victorian photographers delighted in setting up pictures which embraced all the familiar aspects of the ghost tradition as these two pictures show. They clearly illustrate the tremendous public interest in the subject

A remarkable sequence of pictures shot in America of a spirit form materializing. The photographs, which were taken with an infra-red film, cover a period of 30 minutes in which the medium, Ethel Post-Parrish of Pennsylvania, built up a cloudy pillar of ectoplasm into the full figure of an Indian girl, said to be her spirit guide, 'Silver Belle'. The event was watched by 80 witnesses, who could detect no trickery

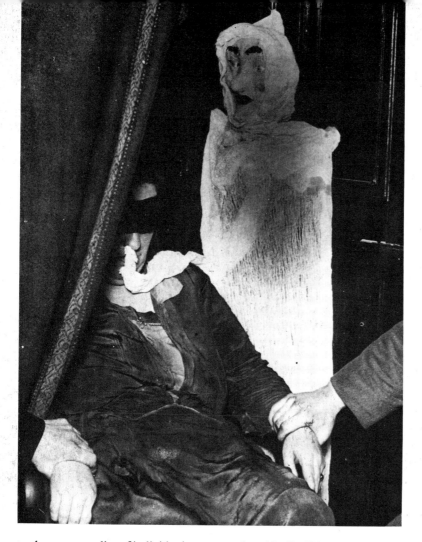

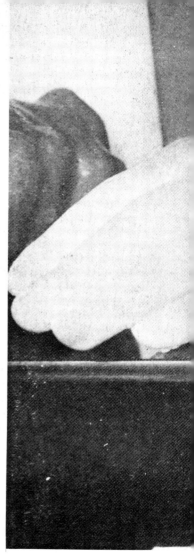

to the many studies of individual cases – such as '*Stella C*' by Harry Price – and documented reports of the whole investigation, such as *Zoar: The Evidence of Psychical Research Concerning Survival* by W. H. Salter.

Perhaps before leaving Spiritualism we should make some mention of an extraordinary development of this period – yet another attempt to prove the actuality of ghosts, but this time by the making of wax casts of the faces or hands of materialized spirits! This technique was invented by the Polish businessman, poet and occasional medium, Franek Kluski, who apparently induced his spirits to plunge their hands into a pail of hot paraffin wax and then to leave thin wax shells or 'gloves' floating in a basin of cold water conveniently placed nearby. His seances were always conducted in very feeble light; there were a number of witnesses who testified that while they did not see the spirit clearly, they could 'hear it splashing the water'. After the seance, a comparison of the wax hands with those of the people present was made and they were always said to be quite different. Later the wax casts were filled with plaster of Paris, and when it had set the wax was dissolved so that the hands could be studied still more closely. Kluski also produced wax casts of two of his ghosts' faces which are reproduced here in their final plaster of Paris

Left: Mrs Helen Duncan's controversial materialization which became known as 'The Coat Hanger Witch'

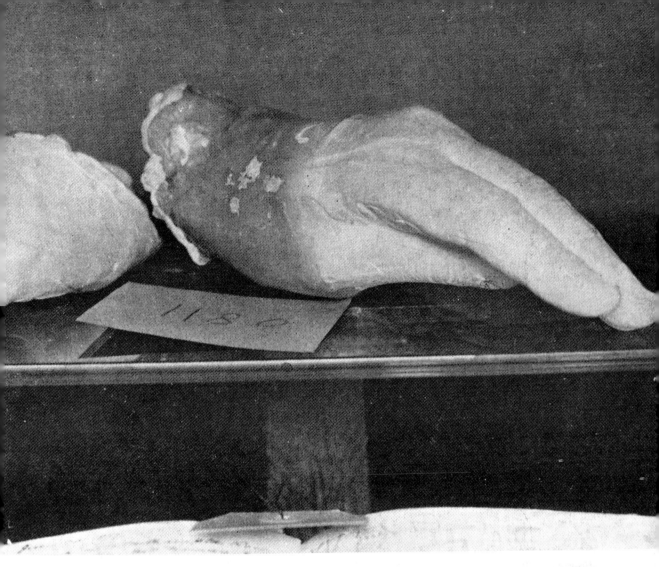

Franek Kluski, a Polish
medium, produced some of the
most extraordinary
materializations in spirit
history. Above: The wax
'gloves' produced by a spirit
dipping its hands in a bowl
of wax and (right) moulds
made when spirits impressed
their faces into soft wax

moulding, along with the casts of some spirit hands. Although one can make wax hands fairly easily in the manner described, no one has been able to prove categorically that Kluski's models were fraudulently produced, particularly as it is virtually impossible for any normal person to draw his hands back through the narrow wrists of the wax gloves without destroying them.

Bizarre though these ghost 'impressions' are, they are considered by some psychic authorities to be secondary in importance to the terrifying animal manifestations which Kluski produced between 1919 and 1923. These took place in Warsaw on a number of occasions and were witnessed by people of the highest integrity, including Professor F. W. Pawlowski of the University of Michigan.

The first creature was a bird rather like a hawk. 'It flew round, beating its wings against the walls and the ceilings,' Professor Pawlowski later wrote, 'and when it finally settled on the shoulders of the medium it was photographed with a magnesium flash – the camera being already focused on the medium and made ready.' There was no possibility, the Professor went on, of the bird having been introduced surreptitiously into the room, or of hiding it after the manifestation. It just appeared and vanished, he said, 'in the way of human phantoms'. The medium also produced a small animal like a weasel 'which ran over the table and smelt the hands and faces of the sitters with a small, cold nose', a big dog, 'with a mouth full of large teeth and eyes which glowed in the darkness', and a 'completely luminous old man' who sometimes accompanied the dog. More terrifying than all these, though, was the *Pithecanthropus* which appeared several times and was like a huge ape with a large shaggy head and a body covered with thick, coarse hair. One anonymous eye-witness described its appearance on the evening it was photographed: 'This ape was of such great strength that it could easily move a heavy bookcase, filled with books, through the room, carry a sofa over the heads of the sitters, or lift the heaviest persons with their chairs into the air to the height of a tall person. Though the ape's behaviour sometimes caused fear, and indicated a low level of intelligence, it was never malignant. Indeed, it often expressed goodwill, gentleness and readiness to obey . . . it was seen for the last time at a seance in December 1922, in the same form as in 1919, and making the same sounds of smacking and scratching.'

Kluski's animal manifestations were not totally unique – other mediums also produced creatures, for example the seal which appeared at a gathering in London when Field-Marshal Lord Wolseley was present – but his are by far the best authenticated. To this day he has never been exposed as a fraud, the photographs of his animals never proved to be forgeries, and there can be little doubt that he deserves the title of 'King of the Mediums' given to him by Dr Gustav Geley, the Director of the Institut Metapsychique International de Paris.

The First World War, with its years of dreadful carnage and death, produced a great number of stories of apparitions seen by soldiers on both sides. This was nothing new in occult history, for tales of phantom armies and the spirits of dead soldiers condemned to haunt the battle-

The terrifying animal manifestations produced by Kluski. Right: The spirit resembling a hawk which settled on his shoulders and (below) the *Pithecanthropus* which threw objects around the seance room – but did not attack anyone

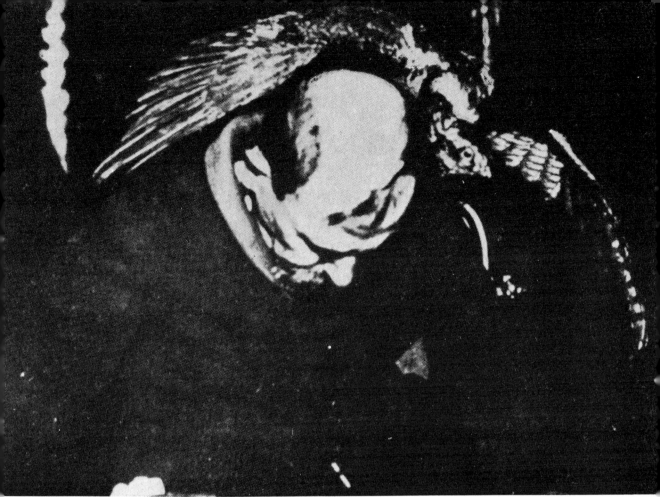

fields where they died have been recorded for many centuries. Plutarch, for instance, tells us that Roman soldiers saw the apparition of Theseus fighting for the Greeks, while in the seventeenth century Lord Nugent described the battle between two phantom armies that was seen and heard on the field of Edge Hill – some two months after the struggle between the forces of King Charles and those of Cromwell had taken place.

The stories of the 1914–18 war have proved to be of particular interest to researchers because many are carefully documented (the *Daily News* ran a column requesting true supernatural stories from the front and was so deluged with replies that two books of collected accounts were later published), and because experts were able to study the material and differentiate between those which were merely the results of exhaustion or hallucination and those which could not be attributed to such factors. The most remarkable of all is surely that of the 'Angels of Mons'.

For years this story of spectral bowmen who came to the aid of hard-pressed British troops at the front was one of the most widely told throughout the world. Eye-witnesses testified to having seen a group of ancient bowmen materialize in August 1914 during the retreat from Mons and scatter advancing German troops with their arrows. The bowmen were actually the creation of the Welsh journalist and writer of super-natural tales, Arthur Machen, who invented the story for the London

GHOSTS

*Evening News* in order to boost morale at the time of the retreat from
Mons. Nevertheless, the story soon became widely held as fact: soldiers
began writing to the newspaper from the front saying they had indeed
seen the bowmen, and in France and Germany, too, the story was
corroborated by troops at the front. That an invented ghost story should
have led to such widespread apparent hallucination is undoubtedly remarkable, for no matter how much Machen insisted that the tale was pure
fiction reports poured in contradicting him. Pictures were also published,
allegedly based on eye-witness acounts, and popular songs about the
'angels' on the side of the British were heard from many entertainers.

Today, so the experts tell us, mechanized warfare has sounded the death
knell of phantom armies; yet stories still persist that the footsteps of
knights resound on certain evenings at Glastonbury, and at Woodmanton,
where the Roman and British armies once clashed, headless war-horses
can be seen galloping swiftly along the darkened valley.

Not long after the war accounts began to circulate about a haunting
which with the passage of time has come to be regarded as the most famous
true ghost story in British history, if not in the world – the Ghost of Borley
Rectory. Linked with this story is the name of the late Harry Price,
certainly the most important psychic researcher and ghost hunter of this
century. It was Price who first described the rectory as 'the most haunted
house in England' and proceeded to study its strange history with pains-

Right: A photograph of Borley Rectory taken shortly after the fire which virtually gutted it. Below: A servant girl at the Rectory points to where the ghost of a nun was seen in the garden

Above: Harry Price, the famous ghost hunter, investigated many cases of ghostly phenomena other than Borley Rectory, including an allegedly haunted 16th-century bed in Chiswick. He and his friend Professor C. E. M. Joad spent a night in it without once being disturbed

Left: Harry Price's 'ghost-hunter's kit' which contained a variety of equipment for testing allegedly haunted places

Right: Excavations taking place in the cellar of Borley Rectory which brought the remains of a human skeleton to light. Below: The extraordinary picture taken at the rectory by a visiting newspaper photographer in April 1944 which, when printed, showed a brick suspended in mid-air as if held by some ghostly hand

taking care. I have recently had access to the hundreds of thousands of words that Price wrote on the subject, his boxes of papers and documents, and the numerous photographs, and there is now no doubt in my mind that for anyone seeking confirmation of the existence of ghosts, this haunting provides the most convincing evidence possible.

The rectory, situated on the borders of Essex and Suffolk, was built in 1863. It was a dark and gloomy mansion full of passages and small rooms and served first as a home to the Reverend Henry Bull and later his son Harry who lived there until his death in 1927. The first stories of supernatural occurrences were heard during Harry Bull's time and concerned a phantom coach-and-horses galloping through the grounds, a girl dressed in white who swept among the trees, and a multitude of strange noises in the rectory. A nun was also said to walk in the house and grounds.

Price, who had already done a great deal of psychic research, exposing a number of phoney mediums and debunking some well-known ghost stories, first went to Borley in 1929. He was so captivated by the legend that the rest of his life was to be absorbed in its study. He set up a research centre in the building, interviewed over 100 people and declared: 'It is probably the best documented and best authenticated case in the annals of psychic research; and the haunting has persisted, to our certain knowledge, for nearly a century.' Piecing together the clues, Price decided that the ghost was the spirit of a nun who had indulged in an illicit love-affair and had been murdered some time in the fourteenth century. Even as he researched, noises broke out again – rustling, bell-ringing, knockings, and objects being thrown through the air. Was the spirit, seemingly a poltergeist, trying to drive off the intruders, he wondered? Price held a seance at which the spirit of Harry Bull was contacted, but nothing definite was learned.

The mansion was then to have two further occupiers: first the Reverend L. A. Foyster and his wife Marianne, relatives of the Bull family, who were driven out by the strange happenings, and finally Captain W. H. Gregson, who renamed it Borley Priory and then saw it gutted by fire in 1939. Price continued to visit the ruins and published his first book on the subject, *The Most Haunted House in England*, initiating the legend which has grown to such proportions today. On one trip a photographer taking pictures of the tumbledown building found on one of his prints a brick suspended in mid-air! (See photograph here). Excavations were also carried out in a cellar and human remains found. Was this the end of the ghost? Harry Price seemed to think so, and published *The End of Borley Rectory* in 1945. After his death in 1948, many theories were advanced about Borley, one school of thought even maintaining that the whole story was Price's invention. This I find impossible to believe of a man who devoted so much of this life to psychic research and scored so many other notable and undisputed triumphs in the field. The ruins of Borley remain today as a silent memorial to one of the most extraordinary modern ghost stories and to the man whose lifework shed much new light on psychic phenomena.

Two other ghost-hunters deserve mention at this juncture because of

The photograph of a phantom monk in Bristol which so intrigued ghost hunter Elliott O'Donnell

their research and their numerous books which the interested reader is recommended to peruse. Elliott O'Donnell was a member of one of the oldest Irish families and according to his autobiography, *Twenty Years Experiences as A Ghost Hunter* (1916), he saw his first ghost while still a student in Dublin, and thereafter resolved to seek them out around the world. In his reports he describes encounters throughout Britain, in America (particularly in San Francisco, Denver, St Louis, Chicago and New York), Canada, Europe, and even Japan! He encountered a variety of spirits, phantom animals and ghostly phenomena, and was responsible for solving a number of strange hauntings. For the purpose of this book I have selected the one case from the many hundreds he recorded which has provided photographic evidence.

The story, which was widely discussed in the 1930s, began following the publication of one of O'Donnell's collections of ghost stories, when he was invited by a Mr A. S. Palmer to visit a haunted house in Bristol. Enclosed with the letter was a photograph which the writer said he had taken of the 'phantom monk' haunting the premises. It had been taken at 2.45 a.m. when a 'curious light' was seen in the room – and when developed produced the monk figure.

Naturally very intrigued, O'Donnell travelled down to Somerset and spent a night keeping vigil with Mr Palmer.

> There was doubt in my mind as to whether a ghost could be photographed, several people I knew having tried to take photographs of phenomena they believed to be objective in haunted houses and drawn blanks – but what took place was amazing.
>
> Nothing happened till about a quarter to three, when we saw a faint glow in cylindrical form on the right side of the room. It seemed to emerge from the wall. On the chance of its being anything superphysical, I stood up and asked if there was a spirit present, and if so would it speak, rap, or give some other token. Though we listened intently we could hear nothing. The light vanished after moving some few feet, and nothing further happening we came away.

O'Donnell went on to investigate the haunting several times more with other witnesses. On one occasion the group was suddenly startled by a member who cried out 'Oh, God, there it is!' and said he had seen 'a dreadful figure' in front of him. 'As no one else had seen anything, I asked him if he could bear being in the dark again for a few minutes,' O'Donnell recalled. 'He assented and I put out the light. We had not been in the dark more than a minute when he called out that it had come again. This time I fancied I saw a reddish light opposite me. I asked if a presence was there, but there was no response of any kind. Nonetheless, I am sure that only the supernatural could have had such a terrifying effect.'

The third member of the triumvirate of famous twentieth-century ghost-hunters, Robert Thurston Hopkins, had a particular interest in ghostly pictures as he was a professional photographer for many years on the now defunct *Picture Post*. He believed implicitly in the existence of phantoms and in one of his books, *Cavalcade of Ghosts* (1956), described

various theories that had been advanced to explain them, including one he particularly favoured that what people actually saw was a 'photograph on the ether'. 'Whenever some great mental conflict has taken place,' he wrote, 'wherever overwhelming sorrow, hatred, pain, terror or any kind of violent passion has developed, an impression of a very marked character has been imprinted on the astral light. So strong is this impression that often persons possessing but the first glimmer of the psychic faculty are deeply impressed by it. But a slight temporary increase of intuitive awareness would enable them to evoke the whole scene.'

During the course of a lifetime he investigated and reported on many of the famous British hauntings, including the strange history of Glamis Castle in Scotland, 'that most haunted and stately old pile, the very embodiment of a castle of romance' as he called it. He also had a bizarre experience in London when he and the poet Ernest Dowson were followed for a period of weeks by a strange figure who had a face like 'a wizened bladder of lard' and carried a gladstone bag in his hand. The man eventually took a room in the same lodging-house as Dowson and just when his continual presence had really begun to unnerve the poet, he was found dead in his bed. His only possession appeared to be the gladstone bag – and when this was opened by the police it was found to be full of *grave-yard mould*! Thurston Hopkins wrote later in *Adventures with Phantoms* (1958), 'I am more than convinced that this wretched errant soul was literally dying on his feet – possibly starving and looking for someone who would take pity on him. But his appearance was so forbidding that no one would heed him. Also I believe that in truth he may have possessed some abnormal gift of hanging on to his body some days after death had really claimed it.'

The story which perhaps most fascinated Hopkins was that of the ghost of Raynham Hall in Norfolk, the seat of the Marquess Townshend. In September 1936 a photographer, Mr Indre Shira, was commissioned by Lady Townshend to take a series of pictures of the Hall. Shira and his assistant were just about to set up their equipment to take some shots of the magnificent staircase when the photographer saw on the bottom flight 'a vapoury form which gradually assumed the appearance of a woman draped in a veil'. Slowly the figure began to descend the stairs, and in great excitement Shira snapped off an exposure. The immediate reaction to the photographer's story was one of amusement – the assistant after all said he had seen nothing – but when the negative was developed it did indeed show the phantom outline of a human figure. Experts who examined the plate agreed that the extra it displayed was not the result of faking. Thurston Hopkins himself studied the picture, which is reproduced here, and similarly vouched for its authenticity. 'It may well be the most genuine ghost photograph we possess,' he decided, 'and no study of the supernatural is complete without reference to it.'

Whole libraries have, of course, been written on haunted castles, houses, churches and ruined buildings, and little purpose would be served by attempting even a modest coverage of them in a book such as this. Consequently I have restricted myself to those which have provided us

Left: The ghost at Raynham Hall in Norfolk which was photographed in 1936 and subsequently investigated by ghost-hunter Robert Thurston Hopkins

with photographic evidence, and the interested reader will no doubt search out other more general collections of stories if he so desires.

Churches, I have found, seem to give us the best documented modern ghost stories: Harry Price himself commented that 'It is a curious fact that the clergy appear to be more frequent percipients or witnesses of psychic phenomena than men of any other calling.' We have already discussed the two most famous historical ecclesiastical hauntings at Epworth and Borley, but there are several more recent stories where ordinary members of the public have had supernatural experiences in churches. One of these was an eighteen-year-old clerk, Gordon Carroll, who photographed a ghostly monk kneeling at the altar of St Mary's Church at Woodford in Northants in June 1966. In a sworn statement made later Carroll said:

> I've always been interested in old houses, churches and castles and I've taken more than a thousand pictures in the last two or three years. Woodford Church is a very ancient place and there was a church there before the Normans came to England.
>
> Anyway I set up my camera – an Ilford Sportsman Rangefinger, which was almost brand new – on a tripod. I used an Agfa CT18 film to take pictures of the coloured windows and took half a dozen other pictures of the church. Conditions were not perfect but I managed to get some very good slides of the windows.
>
> I sent them off to be developed and when they came back I thought the light had got at one I had taken of the altar. But when I put it through the projector I saw I had taken the picture of a monk kneeling at the altar.

Gordon Carroll's photograph caused widespread interest and apart from making headline news in *The People* on 3 July was studied by numerous churchmen and scientific experts who agreed that it was not a forgery and that the kneeling figure seemed to be a robed monk who had probably lived something like 500 years before.

Another priestly ghost was photographed in 1940 at St Nicholas's Church in Arundel, Sussex. The anonymous photographer, a solicitor practising in Arundel, was a man of the highest integrity who had accidentally caught the ghost while taking a shot of the beautiful ornate altar.

Ghosts in churches have also been photographed in Europe as two other examples on the next pages show. The first was taken at the Basilica Domremy in France which was dedicated to Joan of Arc in 1925. In June of that year a Lady Palmer visited the church to see the installation of a Union Jack commemorating the British dead of World War I. After the flag had been hung, Lady Palmer posed for a photograph taken by her companion, Miss Townsend. When it was developed two extras were found, seemingly priests of the time of Saint Joan. The second photograph was sent to me by Mr. H. B. King of March in Cambridge, who took it in the church at Oberdollendorf near Konigswinter in the Rhineland in 1936. 'The picture was taken on a V.P.K. film and I was alone in the church and the pulpit was quite empty' says Mr King, who believes that the figure in the pulpit may be the ghost of one of the monks from the old ruined

The only known photograph of a poltergeist at work – 'The Jumping Stick' which recently so plagued 14-year-old British schoolboy Michael Collinbridge of Barnsley, Yorkshire. This extraordinary affair was investigated by many professional and lay people who testified to having seen the stick suspended in mid-air. The photograph was taken by the Sheffield *Morning Telegraph*

Benedictine monastery sited near the church.

Another ghost story associated with a French church proved to have a logical explanation. For several weeks during January 1920 it was rumoured that a ghost in the form of the Virgin Mary appeared every evening at a little village between Metz and Nancy. A photographer from Paris travelled to the village to picture the phenomenon, and in so doing solved the mystery: certainly a figure appeared in the trees beside the church as dusk fell, but it turned out to be simply a trick of the light among the branches.

Haunted houses have been described in such detail elsewhere as to make repetition in a pictorial history rather pointless. One must however at the very least mention the ghosts which are supposed to haunt the seats of government in Britain and America, 10 Downing Street and the White House. The ghost of Number Ten has always had a real air of mystery about it. Incumbent prime ministers have always denied its existence, yet the rumour still persists. According to legend the spirit is of a prime minister in Regency dress who wanders throughout the whole building. It is said to be benevolent and only appears at times of national crisis. The last sighting was allegedly in 1960 when workmen carrying out renovations saw a misty figure in the garden at the rear. Official spokesmen have, nevertheless, always drawn a veil of secrecy over the matter with a sonorous 'No comment' in answer to all enquiries.

The White House ghost is, however, said to be definitely that of Abraham Lincoln. That the spirit should be his is perhaps only to be expected when one recalls that he was deeply interested in psychic research and even held serious seances in the White House. Mrs Eleanor Roosevelt has recorded perhaps the best story of Lincoln's ghost: 'I was sitting in my study when one of the maids burst in on me in a state of great excitement. I looked up from my work and asked her what was the trouble.

' "He's up there – sitting on the edge of the bed, taking off his shoes!" she exclaimed.

' "Who's up where, taking off his shoes?" I asked.

' "Mister Lincoln!" the maid replied.'

Among others said to have seen the ghost was Queen Wilhelmina of the Netherlands during a state visit, while Harry Truman noted in his diary in 1945, 'The maids and butlers swear he has appeared on several occasions.' Mr Truman himself was disturbed by a knocking on his door one night and finding no one there concluded, 'I think it must have been Lincoln's ghost walking in the hall.'

At the time of writing President Nixon has given no indication of having seen or heard the spirit of his illustrious predecessor.

During my own visits to America, I have heard many stories of ghosts from one extremity of the country to the other, from New York to Los Angeles and from Chicago to New Orleans. I have heard of spirits in Manhattan skyscrapers and in the bayous of the Gulf Coast. Many of these stories have now been gathered together by the ghost-hunter Hans Holzer, whose several books have been published on both sides of the

Churches have for many centuries been a popular place for stories of ghosts, and Europe has been particularly rich in such accounts. These apparitions frequently take the form of a priest or monk, and the majority have been seen close to the altar, often in an attitude of prayer. The photographs here provide four remarkable examples of this phenomenon

Opposite left: The priestly ghost photographed by a solicitor in St Nicholas's Church in Arundel, Sussex. Opposite right: Lady Palmer with two figures dressed in the period of Joan of Arc. Above left: Mr H. B. King's photograph of a ghost in the pulpit of the church at Oberdollendorf in Germany. Above right: The ghost of the Virgin Mary, seen near Metz in France, proved to be the result of light shining through the trees

Atlantic. One of Holzer's most interesting stories, I think, is about an old chair said to be haunted by the spirit of a former owner. It is doubly fascinating because it parallels an English story of a haunted chair, a photograph of which I reproduce here together with the relevant details.

This particular story concerns Bernard and Joan Simon who live in New York and who, a short while ago, bought a strange throne-like chair said to be of Mexican Indian workmanship. 'A few days later,' Holzer writes in his book, *Ghost Hunter* (1963), 'Bernard awoke rather suddenly in the middle of the night from a deep sleep. There was enough light in the small apartment to distinguish solid objects from each other. His eyes were drawn to the chair.

'In it sat an extremely tall man. His back was turned to the observer, but it was clear to Bernard that the man was unusually tall. Before he could get up and challenge the intruder, he had vanished into thin air.' Holzer was asked by the Simons to hold a seance and try to contact the spirit: which was duly done. The spirit spoke through the voice of the medium and told Bernard Simon that his name was Huaska and that he recognized him as his 'son' through reincarnation. 'He had been instrumental in getting Bernard to buy the chair,' Holzer goes on, 'and then was anxious to make himself known. This having now been accomplished, there followed a joyful embrace, and then the Indian was gone. The following days, all knocks and other strange noises that had accompanied the feeling of a "presence" prior to the seance were gone.'

Apart from the numerous individuals investigating ghostly and psychic phenomena, there are a number of organizations working in this area which I think should be mentioned here. The most important by virtue of the wide range of its activities is the Society for Psychical Research which was founded in 1882 by a group of scientists, professors and classical scholars in order 'to examine without prejudice or prepossession and in a scientific spirit those faculties of man, real or supposed, which appear to be inexplicable on any generally recognized hypothesis'. These men simply wanted to bring scientific reasoning both to the age-old mysteries of ghosts, spirits, manifestations, dreams, telepathy, and visions, and to the new religion of Spiritualism.

Soon after its foundation, a number of the members decided to devote themselves particularly to an enquiry into ghosts and apparitions and set about collecting personal testimonies from people who claimed to have seen them. Over the ensuing years a large number of statements were assembled, and the Society found one striking similarity among a large percentage of them: the ghosts had appeared at times of crisis for their beholders. The investigators therefore reasoned that such figures were somehow 'constructed' in the unsettled mind of the viewer and were in fact hallucinations. This theory was expounded in a two-volume report *Phantasms of the Living* published in 1886, but it had also to be admitted that there were a number of reported instances which fell outside the pattern of crisis and had no human explanation.

To this day the Society has continued to collect information and at its headquarters in Kensington, London, there are now something like

This ghost in an armchair, photographed by Mr Sherard Cowper-Coles at Rossal House, Sunbury-on-Thames, has defied all normal explanation

10,000 files on supernatural happenings. A good many of these have of course proved to be hallucinations, tricks of light or plain fraud, but the organization can point to a map of Britain showing the occurrence in more than 700 places of supernatural events which have yet to be explained. In investigating new reports the Society brings the most stringent cross-examination to bear, and the reader may well wish to test any sighting he thinks he has made against the ten basic questions they pose:

1. Could it have been an ordinary person, a shadow, a hanging coat, etc. or someone playing tricks?

2. If you heard ghostly sounds, could they have been normal – a cracking branch, birds, ordinary footsteps, your own breathing, wind in the chimney, or a hoax?

3. Has the place a reputation for haunting? If so, did you know, and were you expecting a ghost?

4. Why are you sure you weren't dreaming?

5. Did you recognize the apparition; if so, how?

6. Did anyone else see it before or afterwards, without either knowing about the other's experience?

7. If anyone else was with you, did he see it? If he did, could the words you spoke have given him a clue to what you had seen?

8. If it was the apparition of a living person, were there any unusual features (e.g. clothes, behaviour) which you later found to be correct?

9. Did you or anyone else who saw it make a written record? If it foretold something – e.g., a death – did you write it down BEFORE the prophecy was fulfilled?

10. Have you had any other apparently psychic experiences? If so, how many and what kind?

A more recent enquiry of the Society into the nature of poltergeists reached less than satisfactory conclusions. One of the principal investigators, Sir William Barrett, found himself convinced of the genuineness of some of the reports, while his colleague Frank Podmore concluded that virtually every one was fraudulent.

A second British-based organization which has recently begun an extensive enquiry into apparitions is the Institute of Psycho-Physical Research at Oxford. Under its director, Celia Green, and four research officers, the Institute has been studying supernatural phenomena for eleven years now, enthusiastically supported by scientists and scholars, not to mention eminent public figures such as Professor H. J. Eysenck, Cecil King and J. B. Priestley. Apart from their work on dreaming, out-of-the-body experiences and extra-sensory perception (ESP), they have begun assembling reports of alleged hauntings and have been struck by the large percentage which occur in the most ordinary surroundings: flats, offices, even the kitchens of suburban houses. Although it will be some time before definite conclusions can be reached, the Institute is tentatively convinced that where mass sightings of a ghost take place, there may well be an unconscious conspiracy, as it were, on the part of the beholders. In other words, telepathy would seem to play a major part. The Institute is currently appealing for reports from the general public

Two extraordinary examples of psychic photography. Top left: A polaroid photograph by Mr Sam Watkins of Virginia, U.S.A. who thought he was taking a snap of his dog and instead found three separate images of his young brother Bill. It is impossible to triple expose a polaroid film, and the bizarre nature of the photograph was further heightened when, a few days later, Bill Watkins was involved in an accident with a car – and just before he was hit was said to have been seen standing beside the road, minus his shirt, and with his hands on his hips

Bottom left: This picture, taken in 1938, of a group of American marines is actually a double exposure – but the man in the centre of the picture who is totally covered by water was to be drowned five years later while attempting to escape from Japanese p.o.w. camp in the Philippines

Top: An image of Marilyn Monroe was found on this photograph taken at the famous actress's crypt by John Myers, an American medium, with his Kodak Instamatic camera

A print of the colour photograph taken in the Australian outback by the Reverend R. S. Blance at Corroboree Rock, 100 miles from Alice Springs, in 1959. The site is known as a spot where aborigines had carried out gruelling initiation ceremonies in the past – but there was no human activity in the area at the time the ghostly figure was photographed

of 'anything seen, heard, smelt, touched or tasted that wasn't really there'.

In America, enquiry into phantasms and apparitions is also going on apace, and it is probably true to say that more practical work is now being done there than in Britain. America has, of course, had its own branch of the Society for Psychical Research since 1885, this being founded in Boston largely as a result of the lectures given there the previous year by the British member, Sir William Barrett.

Among its distinguished investigators have been William James, also president of the English society for two years; James Hervey Hyslop who allegedly returned after his death with messages from the 'other side'; Dr Walter Franklin Price, who studied the famous case of Doris Fischer, the woman possessed by five personalities; and Hereward Carrington, the author of several highly-regarded books on abnormal phenomena.

Probably the most eminent psychic researcher of recent times has been Eileen Garrett, for many years the president of the Parapsychology Foundation of New York, established in 1951. This organization supports scientific investigations around the world and has done much pioneer work in the realm of ESP. It has published several books and leaflets on its work and encouraged much new enquiry into the nature of apparitions.

The Foundation for Research on the Nature of Man, set up in 1964, has been continuing much of the work of Duke University in Carolina which came up with some of the most radical theories on the poltergeist phenomenon. Experts there came to the conclusion that this noisy ghost was not a spirit at all, but a physical force which had its origin in psychological roots. They stated that a substantial majority of cases occurred in houses where young people were reaching puberty, and they felt this budding sexuality could be directly linked with the activities of the so-called poltergeist. They have named this phenomenon psychokinesis or 'mind over matter'. Some weight has recently been added to this theory by the fact that the only known poltergeist occurrence to have been photographed concerned a fourteen-year-old British schoolboy who was beset by a walking-stick while ill in bed. The event, illustrated here, was investigated by journalists, psychic researchers and even stage magicians, but no fraud could be detected.

No survey of spirit-hunting bodies could possibly be complete without mention of London's famous Ghost Club, founded in 1862. Many famous personalities have attended lectures given there by distinguished researchers and authorities on the occult. The Club has also conducted parties to haunted houses and prepared reports on many strange apparitions.

The current president, Peter Underwood, is the author of one of the most comprehensive surveys of apparitions, *A Gazetteer of British Ghosts*, and has heard a great many true ghost stories. In the introduction to his book he writes that 'there are more ghosts seen, reported and accepted in the British Isles than anywhere else on earth.' He goes on, 'I am often asked why this is so and can only suggest that a unique ancestry with Mediterranean, Scandinavian, Celtic and other strains, an intrinsic

The Ghost Club's fascinating photograph of a ghostly presence on the stairs of the Queen's House at Greenwich

island detachment, an enquiring nature, and perhaps our readiness to accept a supernormal explanation for curious happenings may all have played their part in bringing about this state of affairs.'

For me the most fascinating case on the Ghost Club's files is the photograph of the cowled figures on the staircase of the seventeenth-century Queen's House at Greenwich, now part of the National Maritime Museum. The picture was taken in 1966 by a Canadian tourist, the Reverend R. W. Hardy, who was visiting the house with his wife. His photograph was intended to be a picture of the ornate Tulip Staircase, which was deserted at the time; but when the negative was developed, one or possibly two cowled figures could be seen about to ascend the steps. The film was closely examined for signs of faking but none were found. The Reverend professed no interest in the subject of ghosts and turned the photograph over to the Ghost Club which promptly instituted further enquiries. No records have subsequently been found of the house ever having been haunted – although several trusted employees were traced who have reported seeing strange figures near the staircase and hearing the sound of footsteps. (For a full account of this case, see Peter Underwood's *A Host of Hauntings*.)

During the writing of this book, I made several public appeals for 'ghost photographs' – including a broadcast on B.B.C. Radio – and I can only say that I was amazed by the size of the response. It must have seemed to many people that photographs of spirits were an improbability, not to say an impossibility (I know it did to the radio interviewer!), yet in the following months I received dozens of letters and photographs from people throughout Britain, some of which are now reproduced here. All tended to highlight the fact that the old tradition of ghosts invariably appearing in mansions and castles no longer applied: for here were strange figures in flats and suburban houses, in gardens and open fields. Some, I have to say, were clearly the result of double exposure, while others allegedly contained spirit extras which although clear enough to their originators were visible neither to myself nor my colleagues. Others, sadly, did show inexplicable phenomena, but were of such a nature that satisfactory reproduction in this book would have been impossible.

From America, too, came photographs of a variety of phenomena including Christ-figures in the clouds, spirit extras, the extraordinary triple-image polaroid picture of a boy who wasn't there, and the picture taken by a marine of his friend which seemed to presage his death by drowning five years later.

My own researches with camera and sketch-pad have I am afraid only resulted in the little drawing here of what I saw with two companions on a dark winter evening in Chigwell, Essex. The squat figure was almost translucent and we could clearly see the ground floor of a house behind it. Yet, while I do not consider this a totally indisputable sighting, I am convinced at the end of my study of the overall likelihood of apparitions: the evidence from sane and reasonable people over a great many years is just too overwhelming to be dismissed as complete make-believe.

I find myself agreeing too with the great poet and expert on mythology,

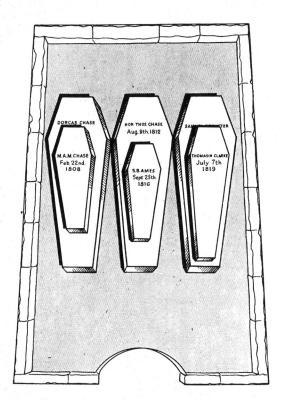

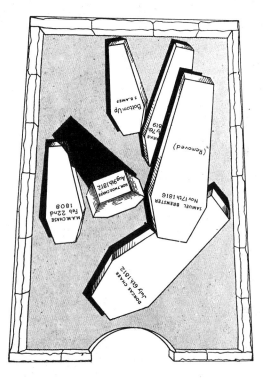

Are the dead trying to reach us from their coffins? These drawings (top left) show the positions before and after some heavy coffins were moved in an allegedly haunted vault in Christ Church, Barbados in 1820. Knocking sounds were also heard recently at the funeral of spiritualist medium Mrs Jane Helen Hughes (left). Several mourners claimed to have heard the strange noises, including the newspaper photographer who took this picture

Above: Londoner Mrs Rosemary Brown, who claims to be in contact with the spirits of several dead composers including Liszt and Chopin. She says they guide her hands to write down and play new compositions (right). Even experts agree these are in the style of the masters

GHOST.
5' Tall.

An impression of the ghostly figure which the author saw during his research for this book

Robert Graves, who when asked a few years ago about the likelihood of ghosts, wrote, 'The commonsense view is, I think, that one should accept ghosts very much as one accepts fire – a more common but equally mysterious phenomenon. What is fire? It is not really an element, not a principle of motion, not a living creature – not even a disease, though a house can catch fire from its neighbours. It is an event rather than a thing or a creature. Ghosts, similarly, seem to be events rather than things or creatures.'

In conclusion, I hope that this book will provide fresh material for discussion and enquiry among students and laymen alike. The camera, it is said, cannot lie; and although we have seen that on occasions it can be used to deceive, there is still much it has captured which defies explanation.

The ghosts on these pages, I venture to suggest, prove that . . .

## PHOTO ACKNOWLEDGEMENTS

The photograph on pp.122-3 is copyright Peter Underwood, The Ghost Club and the Rev. R. W. Hardy
W. Longswood: 27 (top)
S. Gurney: 62-3 (middle top and bottom)
Frank C. Betts: 84 (top)
Mrs. Mellor: 92 (left)
H. B. King: 117 (left)
Church Army: 116 (right)
*The People:* 114
Fujiphotos: 1,120
Mary Evans Picture Library: 9, 11, 20, 21, 23 (top), 28-9, 31, 33, 36, 39 (bottom), 43 (bottom), 47 (bottom), 51, 64, 69, 73 (top and bottom), 74, 82 (bottom)
Radio Times Hulton Picture Library: 10, 31 (left), 44, 45 (bottom), 46, 48 (top), 81 (left), 100, 106, 109 (top)
Paul Popper: 12
Keystone: 13, 121 (bottom)
Michael Holford: 20 (bottom)
Camera Press: 24, 34, 54-5, 124 (bottom), 125
Harry Price Collection: 30 (bottom), 35, 39 (top), 43, 48 (bottom), 64-5 (middle), 83 (top), 89 (top), 94, 102 (top), 108
Mansell Collection: 40 (top)
National Laboratory of Psychical Research: 77, 87 (top)
Photo Press: 91
*Psychic News:* 101, 121 (top)
*Sheffield Morning Telegraph:* 114-5
The Rev. Kenneth F. Lord: 2